God or No God, A 50/50 Chance

"The mysterious realm of religion and the threat of extreme White Christian Nationalism".

Chapters:

1. Is religion such a mysterious realm?
2. Layout current beliefs.
3. Why do we have a God?
4. Where did we get most of these great religions from?
5. The trigger point.
6. Who the Hell Are These White Evangelicals Anyway?
7. What Do You Actually Know About Other Religions?
8. The Native tribes of the Americas had religion!
9. How many Religions are there today?
10. Brief Description of each Major Religion.
11. What actually rules your life if you are not religious?
12. Why we may not believe in God.
13. The Main Religious Divides.
14. What Does Science say about Some Religious Beliefs?
15. Evolutionary Theory or Intelligent Design?
16. What Did Religions Influence?
17. Why can't we do away with religion?
18. Do dying People Hedge Their Bets.

<u>Chapter 1</u>

Is religion such a mysterious realm?

If you unequivocally state you believe in a God, you have a 50% chance of being correct. If on the other hand you flat out state you believe there is No God, you also have a 50% chance of being correct. Logically we must therefore ask, do you just flip a coin because it is a 50/50 percent chance you will be right or how else do we choose what we actually believe or don't believe? Could it be deep down we actually have no idea how our choice regarding God was in fact determined in the first place?

The following assessment is a simple everyday look at how many of us self described "ordinary people" now see religion. This unorthodox view is from a conventional nonspiritual person seeking to understand religion as he approaches the end of his life. Let's delve into the various religions currently available and try to determine if this no religion choice was the correct one or find out why the author did not come to the same conclusion other deeply religious persons have reached?

If you are a nonbeliever in God or a not a Christian, the disturbing question ultimately becomes why do some religions such as the evangelical Christians feel they have to dominate an entire country with their version of faith and totally discredit all other religions? Forcing others into joining your religion is not how most religions are expected to act; faith is supposed to be the driving factor and faith is supposed to be a voluntary decision.

This unwanted forced religion scenario is currently what is driving the American White Christian Nationalism movement so strongly it might eventually destroy America itself? The No God option many are proposing obviously crashes head on with this rising radical extreme religious position! If someone does not believe in any God, why the hell do they have to be ruled by people who just think differently, these are people who believe in some magical being no one has ever seen. Is it just because they go to a particular church on Sunday therefore all others who have a different view point will have to suffer? Is this extreme evangelical attitude really the American approach to religious freedom which has been fought for so many times in the past 225 years?

To be identified as a religious person the overriding aspect is you have to believe in something you can't see or prove. You also have to believe in oral stories told and retold countless times before they were finally written down by hand from these second hand sources from hundreds or perhaps a thousand years earlier. Furthermore, you have to push aside and ignore much of what modern science (2024) can actually prove. In other words, you must rely on pure belief or an absolute faith in what you have been told from ancient history is actually factual. Obviously those last few sentences probably gives you this author's prejudicial starting point about how the topic of religion is viewed.

Many people can believe in both modern day factual science and also a religion which might be several thousand years old. This seems most incongruous to the many who are not religious. It would be logical to assume to be devoutly religious you would have to discount most of modern day science about human evolution and conversely to believe in what modern science shows us you would have to dispel most of the old religious doctrine. To fully believe in both the scientific and the religious creation theories seems a bit bewildering or counter intuitive to many.

Today we are all exceedingly concerned about Artificial Intelligence (AI) becoming too powerful and all knowing. One would have to assume if you asked AI the question "if there really was a God" its' answer should be it was an unknown. So the question was in fact asked from a simplified form of AI called Alexa, on Amazon Fire TV app. The question was asked "was there really such a thing as God", and the answer was as expected. It responded "each person has their own opinion based on religion". So no definitive help with the question is forthcoming from AI, at least this current rudimentary version of AI!

Chapter 2

Layout current beliefs.

The question "is there a God" actually breaks down into many aspects of your own perspective as you will see as you read this book. Most of us logically assume your own family contacts, as you were growing up, were usually the main influencer directing you toward your current beliefs.

Parental forces instill most of your exposure to a religion as you proceeded through the early developmental years. This early exposure could be either highly positive or it might be unnecessarily negative depending on your parent's own personal point of view about religion. As you matured, we wonder how much you were influenced by close friends and eventually your spouse? Did travel experiences to distant lands or attending any higher education institutions present you with any fresh diverse viewpoints about new unknown religions? Finally, the culture you are living in has a huge power to manipulate your perception on how you would relate to any prevalent local religion.

Eventually the final determination all comes down to one simple aspect, faith and only faith. The question ultimately becomes "do you, or can you, believe in something unseen, unfelt, and unheard"? Do you have an unflinching indisputable faith that a God actually does exist or deep down do you really question God's actual existence?

A straight forward definition of Faith is simply a belief in something without empirical evidence. It probably starts out when you are around school age and are influenced by the family rituals you attend such as our many holiday gatherings. Later, because you are a bit older, you are expected to conform to many of the local cultural social norms which tend to be religion orientated. Finally, as a teen you may completely accept the belief system because of the authority it expresses or if you are a typical teen you may outright rebel against such expressed authority. As you mature you may be exposed to many of the inconsistencies between religion and science and become a bit disillusioned about the whole religious aspect of life. Eventually in adulthood you might finally accept the normal local societal systems support of religion without having any further doubts. In this case you trust completely in faith because it now has a higher meaning for you, or conversely you may reject faith in religion altogether. Like most things there are some people who can not firmly decide one way or the other about God and religion!

Growing up as part of the baby boomer generation our family members made sure we attended one of the many protestant branches of Christianity. We went to

Sunday school almost every Sunday, took religious classes and were confirmed as members of the church. For a time, we may have participated as an acolyte, the young person who lit the candles on the altar and led the procession into and out of the church. The previous narrative was a basic and fairly typical church goer routine of the era for a young person. Eventually married and had children baptised in the same church. But in midlife, faith in religion was lost, and now we ask the serious question "is there really a God".

When thinking back, there was always some private questioning about some of the teachings of the church because the stories did not line up with rudimentary knowledge of scientific evidence. Being an inquisitive kid obviously everything will be questioned. It's doubtful you would consider the author a diehard true believer even as a young church going person. Over the years, as more science became available, it became easier to stray further from the so called "true path".

Other factors beside science also seemed to draw many away from religion and most of those would probably have been personal interactions. Unfortunately, some of the people bragging about being religious were some of the worst people many have ever known. They professed to be such good Christians but often showed extremely non Christian personalities and behaviours.

Just like most people, in times of great stress, we would ask for God's help but none ever came, at least none obvious to anyone. They say God answers all prayers, however most often his answer is a definite "no", although you are always left guessing! Some agnostics staunchly believe the NO answer is just a "cop out" because they think there was never a God to hear your prayer in the first place.

After long battles with debilitating illnesses my wife died from Multiple Sclerosis MS and my next wife died from Alzheimer's. Everyone acts differently to these kinds of tragedies, some will get more religious, some will lose their belief in God altogether! This may have been the final straw; the one straw which finally broke the camels back, so to speak.

Now we have the extreme evangelical Christian Nationalism attacking our various religious beliefs and striking fear into many who worry what the next few months will bring to America. These supposed religious evangelicals are unfortunately politically backing an immoral, convicted criminal, and a confirmed want-to-be dictator as their champion flag bearer. That is just a ridiculous action for any avowed true Christian to take. Trump is a proven liar, a criminal, and a conman and not a Christian!

It is the end of May 2024 and Trump has been found guilty of 34 felony counts so he is now a convicted criminal. He has also been found guilty of libel after being accused of rape! He has other outstanding legal cases charging him with trying to corrupt and steal the 2020 election. Unfortunately, his diehard evangelical followers will still follow him no matter what crimes he has done. One would have to assume this does explain a lot about the evangelical Christians and their twisted, out of touch, beliefs. Their grasp on reality has been so distorted by disinformation they are now steadfastly willing to back such an immoral criminal to represent them and their faith.

This is the starting point as we delve more deeply into the question "God or No God". Is it too overly simple for us to state, there really is only a 50/50 chance of being correct, no matter which of the two paths you choose. We shall see?

<u>Chapter 3</u>

Why do we even have a God?

Have you ever wondered where the idea of a supreme God originated? Why does most of mankind continually seem to need this unseen entity in their lives? Is religion actually some mythical relic from antiquity persisting and constantly being promoted throughout our human history or does a supreme God actually exist?

As our early human ancestor's brain developed, their curiosity evolved and we assume they obviously needed an explanation as to why the things around them existed or how did they come to be in the physical form they were now seeing? These earliest dwellers of the planet saw their fellow humans born and die just like other species but they could not explain why. They saw and experienced tall trees, flowering plants, raging rivers, fluffy clouds, hot weather and cold winds but they constantly wondered how were all these things created? The earliest humans obviously had no accurate concrete explanation for the wonders they perceived all about them!

Our ancient ancestors congregated together and eventually larger communal societies developed. Long before science came along with an enlightenment, these early societies had only one possible explanation for any unexplainable happening. They believed it had to be some mysterious unseen and frightening source of immense power that was obviously responsible for all of creations mysteries. Remember it was not that long ago we humans actually believed the sun revolved around the earth and the earth was flat and not round. Science corrected both of these incorrect beliefs.

Earth's earliest inhabitants believed a magical unseen power had created the natural world and gave it life and movement. Eventually our early civilizations finally developed several religious theories to explain the various natural phenomenon affecting them everyday. If providence provided food for them to eat, they assumed there must be some unseen God to thank for this bounty. The creation of these types of unproven superstitions continued and most often were significantly expanded upon over the following centuries.

Many old civilizations identified or created a unique individual god to explain each unexplainable happening they encountered or to help them succeed in important activities. A great example of this is in old Mexico where their Aztec gods were divided into four logical groupings such as for agriculture, weather, war and sacrifice.

In most old civilizations Gods were also envisioned to provide all the things they needed for survival itself. A god of the sea for fishermen. A god of rainfall for early farmers. A god of the winds or a god of fertility and on it went. Ancient Greece had invented hundreds of Gods and Goddesses and the Roman Empire, before the time of Christians, had 12 main Gods and many other minor beliefs. Over 3,000 years ago in ancient Egypt, they believed their human ruler was also a God; well they believed in the almighty human ruler at least as long as the life giving annual flood of the Nile River arrived on time and preceded each planting season. If famine arrived too often the old Egyptian god ruler was cast aside for one who hopefully had more luck with the up stream monsoon rain gods.

For many of the old civilizations it eventually evolved into believing in a single all powerful God who created everything or what we now call a monotheistic belief system. It means for these believers they had cast aside all their other gods but one; for them there is now only one supreme God. From this major adaptation it again branches off into untold variations with each religious sect trying to convert or even eliminate the others.

Some major religions such as Hinduism have more than one God but for our discussion we will use the singular term God to represent all of them.

Chapter 4

Where did we get most of these great religions from?

The area we now call the Middle-East is the most western part of Asia and Asia is where every large religion had its beginning. Most of us already know Jerusalem is considered one of the most sacred sites for three main religions Judaism, Christianity, and Islam so what makes this middle-east area so central to these and other religions.

Why was the Asian continent the birth place of all of todays main religions? Did a God select the location or were there more ordinary rudimentary factors that facilitated this particular geographical setting for religions to get a foothold?

The middle-east area along with China were amongst the oldest centers of human civilizations. Organized civilizations with their connecting roads, written language, and a centralized government, would logically lead to more "group think" and the spread of any new socially acceptable myth such as a religion. These major old extinct empires such as the Sumerian, Assyria, Mesopotamia, Babylonia, Lydia, Phoenicians, Persia, Byzantine, Abbasid, and many others all flourished for centuries at different times in this general area. To add even more influence, just west of the Asian part of the middle-east there existed the old Egyptian civilization and just east of there was the ancient Asian civilization of China which still exists today.

The middle-east is an ideal geographical land area for the transfer of knowledge and the spread of philosophies because if its physical location. This relatively narrow land chokepoint is situated between the continents of Africa, Asia, and Europe, so it meant all overland trade from the three continents would have naturally been funneled through the middle-east area.

Historically this narrow land mass has seen many invading armies pass through such as the Greeks under Alexander the Great, the Persians, the Roman legions, the Ottomans, the feared Mongols, and several others. Overland travel routes had to pass through the area as traversing north above the Black Sea was only a seasonal route, winter travel was not possible. Also traversing this area were the many overland desert caravan routes coming from the east and they eventually went west all across North Africa.

All of these overland trade routes, coming from all four directions of the compass, ended at the eastern end of the Mediterranean Ocean. Here trading ships and powerful ancient navies eventually joined in the expansion of trade to distant ports. The Bosporus Straight, dividing Europe from Asia, provided the commercial sea route between the inhabitants of the Black Sea area and the eastern Mediterranean region.

Trade was extremely important to the growth of these early civilizations and most of the early commerce eventually had to pass through the area we now call the middle-east. Even today we still see the importance of this middle-east trade route using the busy Suez Canal which passes north and south through the western edge of the middle-east.

Major ancient middle-eastern civilizations might have had a leg up on other societies because this is where there seems to be some of the earliest known development of written languages. Obviously this made the spread of written laws, trade agreements, commerce, science, mathematics, and the dissemination of any new religious doctrine possible.

The beneficial side effect of all this multi national trade was an unintended cultural exchange of ideas and social practices. Invading armies also facilitated this cultural exchange but usually in a very brutal fashion. Trade unwittingly facilitated the spread of knowledge and obviously helped pass the word along about each new religion. It seemed trade flourished no matter which invader was in charge of the area at any given time. Invaders came and went, great civilizations came and went, but it seems trade between the people always continued.

We can now see the main religious birthing area for most religions was the advanced, enlightened, middle east which is the far western part of Asia. On the southern part of the huge Asian landmass, on the Indian subcontinent, is where religions like Buddhism and Hinduism began. In far eastern Asia, in closed off China, there were more philosophies being developed by Confucius, Tzu, and others.

It is now obvious why the continent of Asia, which includes the middle-east area and the attached Indian subcontinent, is known as the birth place of all of todays major religions and many long standing social philosophies.

Chapter 5

The trigger point.

What was the catalyst prompting this investigation into the overarching concept of religion and to write down the specifics of this ongoing debate? What triggered this sudden outrage enough to force a modern day examination into God or the absence of God?

During February 2024 there was a TV interview where an evangelical woman was asked why she would again vote for Trump. Her emphatic answer, as she positioned her two hands at a flat level one slightly above the other in front of her face, was as she saw it "at the top of the list was Trump and next down the list was God". Wow, some critical thoughts came immediately to mind, such as "some Evangelical Christian, she doesn't even know the 1st of the 10 commandments". How can this woman consider herself a true Bible thumping Christian with such an obvious distortion of the Bible and its 10 commandments? The same day another MAGA person being interviewed said they prayed to God and He sent them Trump. Really, He sent Trump, what unbelievable ridiculous crap!

For many of us knowledgeable followers of history and politics, those two very dumb statements from two diehard Trump followers struck a sensitive nerve.

Personally, if you were a genuinely well informed religious person, you would judge sending Trump to America as a plague from hell, not a gift from God! The opposing view, which differs from those two radical right-wing republican interviewees just mentioned, is many discerning voters objectively and correctly see Trump as just a lying, rapist, racist, fascist, con man and nothing more. Certainly no where near anything deserving to be revered or frankly even remotely admired, especially by supposed God fearing Christians!

A few short days later a Supreme Court judge in Alabama stated even frozen embryos, before implantation, were actually people so you could not dispose of imperfect or unused embryos or you would be charged with murder. To make matters worse this judge said in a second follow-up interview, he was following God's will and God also created Government.

Those two ridiculous comments from an idiot republican judge didn't sit well either, especially if you were the type of person who isn't sure they believe in any God! This diehard religious Alabama judge was letting his religious belief taint his supposedly impartial judicial decisions. What happened to the so called entrenched American idea of a separation of Church and State; has this founding pillar of America just been pushed aside so one's own personal religious beliefs now supersede even well established American law? Has white evangelical

Christian Nationalism already taken over as this idiot Republican judge seems to think?

After all the above ridiculous crap hit the air waves many concerned citizens started to worry about where Trump's America was headed. Was the rising tide of evangelical Christian nationalism going to be America's final downfall? If you let one religion dictate to the entire nation you will end up with an incredibly polarized country like we see in Iran, Afghanistan, or even Israel!

One ominous tenet of this Christian Nationalist movement is they believe a so called "strong man" is required to help them push through or force their ideological religious view on others. The strong man apparently has to be a fascist dictator for the process to work in their favour otherwise such a change would not be legally allowed do to the restrictions based on the founding American constitution.

It was obvious much more research was definitely required to fully understand the white evangelical Christian nationalism movement! Why would these Christian American citizens sacrifice their own personal freedom and trust the future of America to a dictatorial idiot, just to install their misguided personal religious views?

Chapter 6

Who the Hell Are These White Evangelicals Anyway?

Apparently the word "evangelical" originates from the Greek word for good news. The "good news" for evangelical Christianity is the act of being born again by which you experience a personal conversion guided solely by the Bible.

According to Wikipedia, to be born again is a core belief in evangelical Christian denominations, particularly Methodist and Baptist churches. It refers to a "spiritual rebirth" or a regeneration of the human spirit by the operation of the Holy Spirit and it occurs when one is baptized in water. They believe you have to be born again before you can see or enter the kingdom of heaven because you must have a personal and intimate relationship with Jesus Christ.

Based on this definition, evangelicals would seem to be a small minority of protestants and an even smaller minority of all Christians. One estimate is about 25% of Americans are evangelicals and they constitute the single largest cross denominational religious group in the country. Many knowledgeable people who can do simple math disagree with this high of an estimation of the number of evangelicals! Only about half of America's citizens consider themselves religious to start with so the overall numbers just don't add up! These white evangelicals are supposedly spread out amongst every one of the Protestant denominations such as the Anglican, Presbyterian, Baptist, Methodist, Lutheran, Mennonite, Quaker, and many more, but they tend to be a small minority within most of the mentioned religions.

Now the current problem with this religious sub movement is they seem to be convinced in a belief that only Christians, further concentrated down to only white, born again, Christians should rule America. Meaning, no one else would have any political power except them! This belief is called Christian Nationalism and is Christian identity politics in the extreme.

These people strongly believe their form of Christian religion and only followers of their religion should rule everything. Their proposed overarching ruling power goes all the way from the church up through the family group, further up through other institutions like education, the media, the arts, business, and unfortunately even the Government. We obviously should add this movement is primarily driven by the white race so it is usually labeled the "white" Evangelical Christian Nationalism.

So where does this extreme religious principle leave the rest of us who do not believe in being dominated by an over zealous group called born again Christian

Nationalists? Does it mean if you are not a white "evangelical" you can't be a teacher, a broadcaster, a musician, a business manager, or participate in any level of government? Most Americans do not think the radical Christian Nationalism theory was the true founding father's intension for America, but if Trump gets re-elected these will be the majority of extreme religious morons who will put him back into the White House.

Unfortunately, these evangelicals wrongly feel their faith is increasingly under assault because the country is now more racially diverse and as they see it, more irreligious. They falsely claim what they are doing is in the name of religious freedom when the exact opposite is true. They are actually trying to supress all other religions, especially Muslims, and this suppression also includes other Christians such as Catholics. This is not religious freedom by any definition you may want to use!

Many other American voters think they will be safe from the power excesses of the new dictator! These misguided voters are people who are not diehard evangelical Christian Nationalists but still support Trump and his right wing radicals. However, the extreme uncompromising evangelical Christians will not tolerate any resistance from anyone else once they get into power. They will purge from power anyone who is not a white conservative born again Protestant. This especially includes Catholics, because they think the Catholic God is more like Satan.

These evangelicals firmly believe in the false theory that America was founded by Christians for only supposedly "real Christians" and if you are not a born again evangelical you are not really a true Christian. Once they get into power they will make sure they never relinquish it, which by the way is also Trump's new game plan. America's next civil war might not only be against a dictator like Trump but could be a religious war against White Evangelical Nationalists where no religion is permissible except theirs!

Trump is now the evangelical's hero and flag bearer because he saw an opportunity to corrupt their movement for his own ends. Many of the voting public wonder what kind of disaster would a second Trump victory incite? Will the rest of us who may not be white or not born again Christians have to actually rebel against such a disastrous loss of our constitutional rights and religious freedoms? Most people firmly think all hell is going to break lose in America at the end of 2024 no matter which party wins the election and gets into power. If the right-wing Republicans win in 2024 there will be hell to pay by their new dictator who wants to exact revenge against all who opposed him and if the Republicans lose they won't accept the loss and there will be hell to pay anyway. So get ready America, the second civil war might be just a few short months away!

There seems to be a real lack of understanding what a white evangelical Christian Nationalist actually infers and most people could not accurately describe what the term actually meant, this author included. After some extensive research it was determined that to their faithful followers' evangelical really means Christian dominance in all of American society. Others who are outside this evangelical movement consider the movement a racist, authoritarian, bigot filled, and an exclusive faction. When you investigate the evangelical members in detail, the last description does seem to fit most of the extreme members amongst them.

Recently the state of Louisiana passed a law which mandated the 10 Commandments be placed in every school classroom. The evangelical movement inside the state had pressured the state legislature into passing such a law. This new state directive is against the established law of the land regarding freedom of religion as dictated in the 1st Amendment of the constitution. No law can be passed that tells a citizen to worship a god nor can it specify which god as the Bible's first commandment directs. All citizens are free to worship any god they want, free to follow any religious book they want, or free to follow no god at all, and they do not have to follow any rules from the Christian bible or any other religious writing.

Moral Majority:

Apparently evangelicals now see themselves as a *moral majority* that has been mobilized to counter Satan from taking over all of America. On the other side of the coin if you are an nonbelieving agnostic, you do not believe there is such a thing as a devil or Satan to start with! The evangelicals are against the so called devils agenda of <u>socialism</u>, <u>crime</u>, <u>secularism</u>, and <u>globalism</u>. In reality any racist group such as theirs, sure as hell is not moral nor is it the majority, so let's quickly toss the stupid "moral majority" crap into the garbage heap where it belongs!

Let us examine these four evils the evangelicals seem to fear so much. First is <u>socialism,</u> a form of democratic government which tries to help every level of society. If you take the time to study it, you will see there are many benefits for you personally and it is not the big boogeyman the extreme right wing wants you to believe it is. Socialism is nothing like communism so don't equate the two, they are vastly different. Most existing advanced democratic governments such as in the UK, France, Germany, Japan, Australia, and Canada have some socialist policies that have been implemented to serve the majority of their citizens. Such items as universal healthcare, inexpensive or free childcare, social security for the elderly and many more programs are all socialist policies. Even the USA has its own socialist policies such as food stamps, Affordable Care Act, Medicaid and Medicare, welfare, and social security pensions. If you are using any of these American socialist programs, do you really see anything wrong with using them for your own benefit, most sane people don't! If you believe these programs are ok with you because they help you or your family members, why is the term socialist so feared? It is such a dumb irrational fear when you really think about it!

If you need more convincing about the benefits socialism take a look at Sweden for a realistic examination of Socialism and its help for the average citizen. Sweden has a productive thriving free economy, free higher education, free heath care, lots of vacation time, full pension system and a great childcare system. Everything a normal person would want in their life but it does take higher income taxes to pay for it all. About 20% of Swedes consider themselves millionaires and there are 41 billionaires and that is in a small country of less than 11 million people. Unlike America, in Sweden everyone contributes equally, repeat *EQUALLY*, and everyone benefits *EQUALLY* so all of the countries wealth is more evenly distributed. America should be so socially and financially balanced and frankly, so lucky!

The next evangelical fear is <u>crime</u>. Let's face facts here, you are always going to have crime; it has been around since the beginning of recorded history, Christians should remember the story of Cain and Abel. Currently the level of crime has been going down in the USA, not up as Trump constantly and wrongly insists. Also as we get higher employment under Biden we can see the crime rate goes down further. The evangelical extreme version of religion, all on its own, would have absolutely no effect on crime one way or the other.

Third is their fear of <u>secularism</u>. Secularism means religion is not involved in governance in any way, but religion itself is protected in all other aspects of daily life. It ensures all faith-based ideas, religious ideology, or other such superstitions are not allowed in the decision making processes of any government policy. In other words, it means a definite separation of church and state as the founders of America had originally intended. All government policy must be based on facts, scientific evidence, and logic and not on any particular religious' ideals. Secularism stops government from favouring one religion over another religion or over nonbelievers; it guarantees religious freedom for everyone in the entire country. You can easily see why evangelical Christian Nationalists would be fanatically opposed to such religious freedom for all the rest of America's citizens.

Lastly we have the evangelical fear of <u>globalization</u>. At first glance it is difficult to see why any country, which is the richest on the planet by trading with the entire globe, would be against anything called globalization. Although some isolationists see globalization as creating a wider divide between the wealthy and the rest of us. The rich see globalization as a way of removing borders that prevented a roadblock to their wealth generating agenda. Our old entrenched religions had become a bit of a refuge from the effects of modernization of trade and the constantly changing cultures that globalization had brought to America. However, the evangelicals do not see the benefits on the global stage of better living conditions for others around the world, reducing the chances of world war, and all the new cultural experiences and benefits a multicultural society can bring to America. Evangelical American isolationism is a disaster for both the nation's economy and for all of society!

Immigration:

The slow culture change evolving from recent immigration has created a white American backlash and increased national identities to the detriment of new immigrant arrivals. The evangelicals fear this loss of tradition and having their social status disturbed because they are starting to feel culturally displaced. The American "melting pot" strategy was good enough for their white Christian immigrant predecessors to follow and flourish but now it has to be stopped for all others who are not exactly like them in their skin color or their preferred religion!

Overall these evangelicals also believe they face threats from non-Christians, non-whites, and of course all new immigrants. Sounds like these morons are afraid of their own shadow and need to have something or more likely, someone, to blame for their own short comings. Any available visible minority target is fair game to blame for their misguided unfounded fears! The more visible these non-white nationalities are, the easier they become targets for this racist anti-immigration mentality. Any mention of war, increased immigration, or economic uncertainty panics them and encourages them to more extreme behaviour.

Evangelicals are not and must not be considered religious patriots as they do not believe in the founding ideals of America. Being overly nationalistic they are now only loyal to their white Christian populace and not the country as a whole. Despite all the above religious rhetoric they are basically all about power and keeping all the power in the so called "right hands", meaning only their fellow white protestant born again Christians. Trump, the racist and now convicted criminal, constantly preaches such intolerant nonsense at every one of his election appearances.

To this end, evangelicals love Trump because he brags about protecting their faith and their race, and he has dragged the entire Republican party into this fascist undemocratic fold. The original GOP have now disappeared and have been replaced by the dictatorial Trump cult.

A true democracy demands we share power, so real democracy is directly opposed to the fascist white Christian Evangelical movement. The white evangelicals want to make sure America does not turn its back on religion by allowing colored people to immigrate into the country or allowing other religions to stand in parallel to Christianity within America's borders. We sincerely have to ask, "is this false Christian Nationalism theory what freedom loving America is now all about"? Most of us don't think so, at least we hope not!

When it comes to Trump many of the evangelicals can't see the forest for the trees. Trump was criminally charged after 4 grand juries of his peers, in 4 different states, decided he had broken the law. The evangelicals do not believe that any of the 91 state and federal criminal charges against Trump are actually legitimate charges and he will be found innocent. That should give us all pause to worry as these people have no grasp on reality what so ever.

Many of Trump's co-conspirators have already pled guilty and have implicated Trump in their many crimes. Evangelicals don't seem to care that their religious flag bearer has several divorces, had sex with a porn star while his wife was home with a new baby, says it is ok to grab strange women by the pussy, lies about immigrants, and has been found guilty of defamation. There are several cases still outstanding indicating him in sexual assault as well. He is not a great business man and has been found guilty of business fraud in New York State. He is a con man as we found out in his Trump University scandal. He illegally used funds from his own charity for his personal use. Now, like the shameful huckster he is, he has gone from selling overpriced beef steaks to selling Bibles to his gullible followers. We can now add he is a convicted criminal as the New York jury recently proved. So where are all these evangelicals hiding their true Christian morals, that might be the big question to confront them with when they say they back Trump! We have to state the obvious again, Trump is definitely not a true Christian by any definition and never has been!

We don't have to wonder what kind of disaster would happen if the Trump cult and his evangelical Christian Nationalists did get control of the government by helping Trump get elected in 2024. He has already pretty much stated what will occur if we only took the time to listen!

The following section is taken from my book "<u>Are Americans out of Touch with Reality</u>". (2024)

What will Trump the Dictator do?

Apparently Trump has been secretly infatuated with Hitler for several decades, his first wife said he kept a copy of Hitler's speeches in a cabinet next to his bed. All fascist dictators follow the same steps from the common authoritarian playbook and all the steps share similar features with only slight changes reflecting the unique specifics of their own country. Being overly nationalistic, fascists seem to yearn for a past that has been long gone. They may want a return to things such as a more rural past or a purer view of the population like it used to be before recent immigration and they want to bring the old bygone ways back. His slogan of Make America Great Again really means to his followers Make America ***White*** Again.

Dictators are always supported by large groups of armed militias who are reinforced by their own imagined grievances and blame all their shortcomings on others. Each fascist leader tries to delegitimize the other political parties they are competing against and all fascists categorize these political opponents as some kind of demon organization. They try to convince followers their specific group are the only true Americans while all the rest of the population are only vermin and not really human enough to be real Americans.

Fascists launch unending attacks on the free press and expound their own propaganda machine as the only viable source of real news. They push their own false image of great masculinity while at the same time try to represent they are poor innocent victims of the current government's underhanded attacks and have a collective grievance against all existing authority. The most worrisome aspect is they foster the notion of ethnic cleansing and insist all racial contamination must be stopped. At the same time, they promote the ridiculous idea that all the so called deep state supporters in the government must be routed out and destroyed. It is frightening to observe Trump actually using these same fascist NAZI corrupt authoritarian phrases and techniques, is it not?

Those tried and true dictator actions are just some of the standard fascist playbook ploys and so far Trump has followed these schemes to the letter. It stands to reason that Trump will continue to follow the playbook and do what all other dictators have done, so let's take a look at the coming disaster!

It now looks like Biden/Harris ticket will have just enough third party candidates in the presidential race to cause them to lose the 2024 run for president to Trump. So what would happen in the USA if Trump wins in 2024 and he declares himself the fascist dictator for life.

First he will scrap the Constitution and outlaw all other political parties. He has specifically said he would do that and that's just what Hitler, Trump's hero, did once he was legally put into power in Germany. Trump will first fire many of the FBI and the Department of Justice personal and quickly insert his own fanatical followers. They have already drawn up the list of people to insert into the new fascist government. We know Trump will follow the exact same steps as he has even said so publically, so we shouldn't be too surprised when it actually happens.

Trump will act just like Hitler who converted his Black Shirt militia into his own retribution squads to take harsh revenge on all his political, racial, legal, and other perceived enemies, either real or imagined. An important group in the Nazi takeover of Germany was Hitler's Protective Squad or SS. This group was an elite collection of radical misfits from the original Black Shirts militia who actually became the private army of the Nazi party. These goon squads of SS became even more important than the original street fighters, later called Storm Troupers or SA. The existing American white racist militias will undoubtedly be quickly formed under hand picked racist leaders to be Trump's private SS army. Can you imagine a ridiculous clown like congressman Jim Jordan running this new group of SS terror thugs; YUK?

Along with the SS in Hitler's Germany we saw many revenge tasks were carried out for the fascist dictator by the secret state police called the "Gestapo". The much feared Gestapo were given enormous power to arrest, jail, and abuse ordinary citizens who had no judicial protection. When you think of the disgusting Gestapo do the names "Oath Keepers" or "Proud Boys" come to mind, disconcerting isn't it? Can you envision an unhinged crazy buffoon like Marjorie Taylor Greene controlling this group of murderous Gestapo misfits; YUK again? It is a very scary thought to imagine that America could actually descend down to such a level of absurdity and stupidity, but it's actually not a hypothetical prospect any longer! Come January 2025 it really could happen!

Once back in power, Trump will order the arrest of all elected democrats including democratic judges, all union leaders, and all real journalists. His next act will be to close down the free press and any factual television stations or truthful internet systems. Fascists will go as far as replacing all non cult police chiefs, state legislators, city councils, and even school boards with their fanatical fascist Trump followers. American kids will be soon indoctrinated to turn in their parents to the new American Gestapo if they stray from Trump's fascist doctrine. Within 6 months, Trump's MAGA (Nazi) party will be the only political party and democracy and freedom will be officially dead in America.

Once his freedom loving democratic enemies have been neutralized he will next eliminate the blacks, the trans, the gays, the Muslims, and any other American group he dislikes or he feels threaten his total hold on power. How he will eliminate them is a very disturbing question? Will we actually see re-education camps like they have in China or murderous concentration camps like Auschwitz right here in America, amazing as it sounds it sure looks that way! We must remember that 74 million Americans voted for this creep last time, even after his disastrous term in office, so he still has a huge unthinking and uninformed cult following out there!

The big unknown in Trump's new America is what will the military and the various National Guard units do while all this fascist political rebellion is going on? The military personnel all swear allegiance to the Constitution just like Trump supposedly did, but he just ignored it completely. Will American military units have to now swear allegiance only to Trump, what if they don't? What if some military units stay loyal to the republic while others defect and swear their loyalty to Trump the de Führer? Does America fall into civil disobedience or outright civil war? Do we end up with armies from red states fighting blue states? Do America's beautiful cities end up looking like the bombed out and demolished Gaza strip? Do states like California or New York leave the union rather than stay and be dominated by a fascist thug like crazy Trump? Remember a civil war tends to be the most destructive, deadly, brutal, and horrendous kind of warfare. If you are currently in the military you had better think twice before you vote for a dictator like Trump as your safe home and your family's life might depend on keeping him out of office.

The financial fallout resulting from an election win by a declared fascist dictator called Trump will be a truly scary event and the disastrous consequences will impact everyone, no one will be spared! America relies heavily on foreign investment to buy its government bonds to finance America's deficit and also to help finance the stock market. Remember all investors seek a stable secure environment and do not like uncertainly; Trump's goon squads will surely disturb the financial tranquility of America. Will these foreign investors still believe in the security of America as a safe place to put their investment money if the country is in the middle of a civil war or public rebellion; not bloody likely?

America's credit rating will crash and interest rates will soar! Foreign manufacturers will want to receive cash up front before they ship their goods to America. The American dollar may slip away from being the recognized stable world currency and there may be a demand to pay back the trillions of debt that are owed by America to foreign companies and countries.

If you don't like Biden's 3.36% inflation you really won't like dictator Trump's 50% inflation that keeps going up every month that the Trump dollar falls in value. Your private pensions and 401K will evaporate. You had better think twice before giving all your power over to a fascist dictator because the real world will not like the resulting financial upheaval and neither will you.

Most Americans do not follow their countries foreign policy at all, so they will not appreciate what the negatives of having a fascist dictator running the country will entail. He was the laughing stock in the rest of the world the last time he was president and we would expect he would be even less respected if he wins again. Trump just loves all his fellow strong dictators so the rest of the free world will have to watch for strange alliances which might eventually put America directly in harms way.

Trump thought nothing about adding punishing unwarranted duties onto products arriving from America's closest allies so they obviously retaliated by adding duties onto American products sent to them. These expensive duties are eventually paid by the citizens of both countries, so there is really no winner, just losers. Now he says he will put a 10% duty on everything coming from China. Don't be fooled, you will pay that 10% and no one else. China will obviously retaliate and American business and workers will suffer!

Trump is Putin's best friend so he will help the Russian dictator. If Trump wins there will be no weapons sent to Ukraine so the invading Russian army will eventually defeat Ukraine and put all of Europe under threat of a further Russian invasion. Other NATO countries will not be able to count on America any longer, so peace in the world will be in dire jeopardy again. If you like living in a safe secure country, you had better think twice before voting for Trump and his fellow republican fascist thugs.

Many of the GOP running for federal seats in 2024 have openly said they want Social Security eliminated, Medicare and Medicaid eliminated, Obamacare (ACA) eliminated and no replacement has been proposed for any of these vital programs. You know Trump will go along with these radical conservatives just so he has more money in his budget to pay his deranged gang of misfits. All you Veterans, seniors, disabled, and 40 million on Obamacare had better think twice before you vote for Trump and his GOP mafia. He said in 2016 that he would bring in a better cheaper Obamacare, but we all know he did not have any plan in place, so his repeal and replace for ACA was just another one of his thousands of lies; we should expect no different this time.

Perhaps the biggest loser if Trump gains power will be the environment itself. The GOP have stated all, not some, but ***all regulations*** regarding Global Warming will be rolled back and eliminated. The push for Green Energy will be stopped dead in its tracks, just so his fossil fuel election contributors can continue to reap huge profits at the expense of the planet. Again we see Trump and the rest of the power hungry GOP think only of themselves and care so little about mankind's future. Actually the GOP have now stated they want all regulations removed on everything so even pollution controls that protect our freshwater will be removed along with safety regulations that protect workers. It looks like America will revert back about a hundred years and our health and our environment will again be at the whim of uncaring, everything for profit, large corporations.

Many non-Trump people still hold out hope he will be convicted on all or most of the 91 criminal counts currently being prosecuted against him and he will be in prison by November 2024. That wish will definitely not happen! Even when convicted, and because he is guilty he will be convicted, there will be appeal after appeal issued by his lawyers and most will slowly make their way eventually to the snail paced, GOP dominated, Supreme Court. Once the case is at the Supreme Court, his hand picked crooked judges will have the final say but all these judicial appeals processes will take several years. If he does get elected before a final appeal verdict is rendered, he will just pardon himself or throw out all the unfinished cases because he will have taken total control of the justice department. He has said if he is elected, Christians will never have to vote again, so that is proof he will end democracy in America. If America stupidly elects Trump again in 2024, we are stuck with him permanently! Not just for the next 4 years, but permanently! His rise to brutal dictatorship will begin immediately as well as implementing the promised racist evangelical Christian Nationalism policies.

If you are still in doubt as to whether Trump is a fascist dictator in waiting, just go online and look up any article defining the steps of the well used "playbook" to become a fascist authoritarian dictator. You will immediately recognize Trump sitting there secretly accomplishing each step in the fascist playbook, laughingly checking them off one at a time.

In his recent speeches he has even been using the exact same buzz words that the murderer Hitler himself used. Trump calls out his perceived enemies as "vermin", exactly what Hitler called them. Using the term vermin is how you dehumanize your opponents so that it becomes easier to use violence against them. Trump continually points out, in his view all immigrants are "poisoning" the purity of the nation's bloodstream, just the same way Hitler said things about any non white, non Christian, members of the German race. This kind of extremist rhetoric is just more intentional underscoring and race emphasizing to stir up the white racist movement. More proof Trump is a carbon copy of Hitler himself; why can't the voters recognize this fact themselves?

Many trusting Americans don't believe Trump has enough votes to become a dictator despite the fact many

Republican primary voters actually want Trump to be a dictator after they elect him and they have said so quite openly. As unbelievable as this seems, this diehard core of the evangelical stupid GOP actually wants fascism to rule America.

Unfortunately, too many average Americans still feel they are safe because Trump followers are not the majority of American voters. However, as we saw in Germany in the 1930's you really don't need a majority to impose a dictatorship. In Germany it has been calculated only about 1 in 70 people wanted a fanatic Nazi to be their leader but the rest went along just to join the crowd or to avoid being singled out as nonbelievers. It has previously been shown as few as 10% of the voters throwing their diehard support behind the fascist insurgent can create the absolute collapse of a democracy. In many countries, fascism has eventually lead all the way down into horrific barbarism. If a diehard 10% are all that's needed for Trump to win the primary and during the general election the rest of the GOP vote republican as usual, the result in 2025 is we will end up having a fascist dictator running America. Again it must be stated, if America wants to remain a democracy, Trump must not get elected and his current fascist group of GOP cult followers must be thrown out of office as well. The fear is the average American may not actually appreciate how utterly important the 2024 election has become for America's freedom and their own well being!

Again, we have to ask evangelicals, "if your evangelical Christian religion is so wonderful what are you so afraid of"? If only about half of America even admits they are religious at all, why should the other half of the nation have to bend to your minority white nationalist wishes? Christian Nationalism is definitely not what America stood for all these many years!

One recent poll on religion has surprisingly revealed only about 75% of Americans even have a religious preference. Only about 50% of Americans said religion was even important to them, or indicated they belong to a church or regularly attend religious services. About 29% said they are atheist, agnostic, or don't have any religious preference at all. Given these statistics the evangelicals are far from being any kind of majority and certainly not a moral majority by any stretch, period!

The current weakening of organized religion seems to be an ongoing trend! Is it caused by a general apathy about religion in general or is some other factor driving the shift away from organized religion. Is this weakening of religion following the other such trends like a widespread drifting away from all organizations and could the preponderance of online gaming, online social interaction, and other such online activities be a hidden cause? Have these so called "social internet programs" finally made us less sociable? Has the recent explosion in scientific findings irrefutably removed the Bible's creationist mysteries, which previously only religious faith had been able to answer? Are there other religions out there which are more meaningful in todays fast paced scientific world or are all organized old religions now truly redundant? Young people are now so firmly engrossed in todays online technology it is a wonder they see anything or anyone else.

National Church:

The USA does not have a national religion despite what the evangelicals proclaim. The beautiful Washington National Cathedral which is part of the Anglican religion is open to all people with no restrictions. It was constructed to be a house of prayer for all people and institutions of learning for the promotion of religion, education, and charity. It was to be a national shrine and a venue for great services much like Westminster Abbey in the UK. It has often been referred to as "a house of prayer for all people", the "national house of prayer", and a "spiritual home for the nation". It has been a temporary home for several congregations in need of an emergency place of worship including a Jewish synagogue. If all of America was supposed to be purely part of the evangelical religion it would logically have been established in this fantastic religious facility, which it was not! There is definitely no national religion and also no national church!

In God We Trust:

Finally, the saying **"In God We Trust"** needs some clarification! We hear this motto a lot and many Americans assume it has been around and widely used since the founding of America. This is factually incorrect. The saying first appeared, in any meaningful way, more than half way through the Civil War in 1864 when it was applied to the new two-cent coin so the nation would let the world know what the North stood for. It gradually faded from civil war memory until the 1950's when it was resurrected and used as a psychological counter to the growing communist threat and was again brought back to life by president Eisenhower. In 1955 the Congress ordered the old obscure phrase to be put on all paper money.

Many times there have been legal actions taken to try to remove the phrase from the currency and also to remove "under God" from the Pledge of Allegiance" but eventually it was deemed not to be worth the fight as a symbol of a separated church and state. Some truly believe that the phrase had lost any true religious significance so why bother.

Now we have the evangelicals trying to push the idea that America has always been a religious nation and was founded to serve God and unfortunately only their version of a Christian God. Obviously their knowledge of history has been usurped again as that belief is incorrect as well. Several of the founding fathers were not really Christians. People such as Thomas Jefferson, John Adams, and Benjamin Franklin viewed Jesus as a great teacher but was not the son of God.

We see in the phrase, "in God we trust", that it never mentions which God or could it really mean many Gods. If it was such an important issue for the founding fathers why is the word God never mentioned anywhere in the Constitution and also no overriding American national religion has ever been declared. Article VI of the Constitution says that "no religious test shall ever be required as a qualification to any office or public trust under the United States". The first amendment to the Constitution also says "Congress shall make no law respecting an establishment of religion, or prohibiting the free exercise thereof". Thus we get the definitive separation of Church and State as the founding fathers had intended. So now evangelicals want to do away with the First Amendment and part of the Constitution just to shove their Christian Nationalism religion down everyone's throat!

Immigration:
Immigrants are the backbone of America whether evangelicals like it or not! Everyone, and we mean

everyone, in North America actually came from somewhere else; that also includes the First Nations peoples as they came over from Asia several thousand years before the European white man arrived. Every American evangelical, especially the white ones, has an immigrant family somewhere in their history or they would not exist here in America, so why are these descendants of immigrants now so anti immigrant? The only answer has to be they are just racist in their outlook!

With the low American birth rate, if there were no immigrants, America's economy would shrivel up and die. A nations population must grow faster than its death rate or the overall economy will stagnate and weaken. Given these facts why are evangelicals so afraid of immigration here in America? It makes no logical sense! Many refugees have arrived on America's shores not only for survival but also for the religious freedom that was promised. Now evangelicals want to rescind that religious freedom and replace it with a forced conversion to their version of evangelicalism.

Over the centuries many people from varied societies have fled to America for religious freedom:
- First nations peoples established and followed their own religions
- Puritans fled Europe to America seeking freedom to follow their religion
- Mormons fled west to avoid persecution from others

- Mennonites and Quakers came to be free to follow their religions
- Irish came to avoid starvation and follow their Catholic faith
- Jews came to flee Nazi annihilation and follow their Jewish faith
- Hungarians came to flee the Soviet crack down and follow their faith
- Cubans came to flee communism and follow their catholic faith
- Chinese came to flee communism and follow their chosen religions
- Vietnamese came to flee communism and to follow their religions
- Italians came to flee poverty and follow their catholic religion
- Germans came to flee the Nazis and follow the Lutheran religion
- Pakistanis came to flee poverty and follow their Islamic religion
- Indian Sikhs came to be able to follow their faith without persecution
- Japanese came to flee dictatorship and follow Shinto or Buddhist religions
- Chinese Uyghur fled to be free and follow their Muslim faith
- Burma's Muslims fled persecution from Buddhist Myanmar government
- Ukrainians came to flee the Russians and follow Eastern Orthodox faith

Obviously there are countless other groups of refugees and immigrants from many more countries who all came to enjoy the religious freedom that America had represented. Now there is a massive effort to destroy all the beloved promised religious freedom just to appease the evangelical religious right.

The End of a Free America:

The evangelical Christian Nationalist movement is a minority in America. They want to dominate the entire country with their version of religion at the expense of all other religions and they make no pretense about it. This sounds just like the chaos religions have been causing since they first arrived on the scene many millennia ago. Now the evangelicals have attached their religious wagon to the first dictator that has emerged in America. Trump has repeatedly stated that if he is elected there will never be another free election in the USA. Trump and his evangelical followers will ultimately destroy America and after its downfall most other democracies will be put into perilous positions to defend themselves from tyranny as well. If Trump and the evangelicals do get into power, America's future regarding freedom of all religions or freedom to believe in no religion will surely look bleak to most rational people!

Chapter 7

What Do You Actually Know About Other Religions?

Because you grew up and were raised under one religion usually means you know little or nothing about your neighbor's religion. Likely your uninformed assumptions about other religions are not accurate at all. Did you ever attempt to learn anything factual about any of the other faiths, most of us don't? Some of the old extremely strict religions openly forbid or at least strongly object to you studying any other religions. One would logically assume they are afraid you might find flaws in your current chosen faith and be enticed to switch to a new religion if you actually studied one or more of the many other religious beliefs.

Some overly devout people spend their entire life studying their one chosen religion. There are many names or titles for these overly religious dedicated people, they are often referred to as monks, clerics, holy men, shaman, nuns, priests, or religious scholars. Most of these people remain completely immersed inside their religious studies, they remain cloistered together, and many never do anything else but study all the intricacies of their chosen faith for their entire life.

These devoted clerics delve into their religious teachings and their religious books and texts, such as the

Quran or the Bible, and dissect every single word to understand the full meaning of what was written so long ago. One could seriously assume, if you have to constantly study and reinterpret every single word of your chosen religious text, perhaps you might reasonably conclude these religious scholars didn't know what the hell they were talking about in the first place! For us outsiders, who are not part of their religion, it is obvious we have little knowledge or little interest in what others believe or why they might believe in their chosen religion.

Most of us just follow along and attend the church of our parents and by doing so we are slowly indoctrinated into the same faith. Some of us have to change religions when we marry someone of a different faith and they or their family insist we join their church and forgo ours. Some of us who face major disasters such as participation in warfare may join the faith of our fellow soldiers or our close allies and sometimes because of the horrors of war we lose our faith altogether. Some inquisitive people investigate their religious options by attending religious services of many different faiths and dissect and study what they learned, ultimately deciding which faith seems to suit them best.

Once a person's faith is confirmed, many of us are expected by our chosen religion to try to convert all those who took a different path. In many religions it is part of their religions' doctrine and becomes their duty as a member of the congregation to convert others to their faith. We all have had Mormon missionaries knock on our door or we have seen people dressed in monk style robes at the airport from the mystical sect of Hinduism called Hare Krishna, who are handing out their literature and asking for donations. Similar missionary activities are carried on to some degree by all religions. These missionary activities are mandated by their religion and must be followed by their devotees. To "grow the faith" is a prime tenet of every religion, be it global or just local.

Chapter 8

The Native tribes of the Americas had religion:

Were there any religions here in North America before the white Europeans arrived after 1492 to spread their long held religious beliefs? Did the widely dispersed native tribes each follow their own unique religion or was there a common theme amongst them all? Did the original foreign white invaders or the settlers that eventually followed them ever bother to find out about the native religions?

Unfortunately, what we do know is there was always a push to have the indigenous beliefs or their religions suppressed and supplanted by the new white invaders religion. Many of the western hemispheres first European explorers and conquers were accompanied by missionaries from various European religions and it was part of their exploration or crusade to convert as well as to conquer the indigenous peoples they encountered. This unfortunate specific religious conversion approach was carried out by every invading nation throughout all of history and all around the world and not just in the Americas.

Prior to the white mans invasion of North America there were about 600 identifiable first nation tribes in Canada and another 560 or so in the USA. Their common spiritual traditions usually included the presence of creation stories, fear of supernatural imposters, and the importance of a sacred person or a spiritual organization or place. From aboriginal generation to generation, these creation tales were verbally passed down explaining the origin of the earth, moon, sun, stars, animals and humans. These individual tribal tales carried with them lessons regarding how to use our human relationships to cherish the environment and how to maintain respect for all of nature they saw around them.

These smaller unique tribal societies each evolved independently to have their own "indigenous religions". Localized religious tribal beliefs were usually orally transmitted and became a major part of everyday lifestyles. Their ceremonies most often included beating drums, wearing costumes, and participating in group dancing to depict a long ago story and to ask the Gods for good hunting and full crops. Many tribes had sacred objects they carried with them much like the Christians of today with their crosses hung around their neck. Daily activities such as hunting, fishing, farming, tribal membership, and other activities were intermingled with their own unique tribal spirituality.

Similar to the much larger current worldwide religions there were some obvious similarities between the aboriginal faiths as well but there was no single overarching "indigenous religion". Also similar to the middle east there was some trading amongst tribes and there would have been exposure to each others religious beliefs. Many tribes held the same basic idea of a Creator, Great Spirit, or Great Power and this powerful being created the world and everything in it. Spiritual power was also present in many if not all living things and also in some ritually significant locations. Their deities were basically good Gods and must be appreciated and it was also believed they could be dangerous if they were not properly respected.

Perhaps we should be regarding these first nations people as the first true environmentalists. They were centuries ahead of the current group of ecological activists who now finally have respect for nature and are fighting an uphill battle trying to save our fragile planet.

The many different tribes believed a variety of "afterlife" theories. Some thought the afterlife was a joyous and peaceful place where passed ancestors and animals can still visit and communicate with the living. Some tribes believed the spirit travels to the happy hunting ground, although that might only be a distorted movie myth. Some believed in reincarnation where they would come back as an another person or animal. There are many variations on the spirit, or soul, and an afterlife and it is defined differently by what each tribe believed.

<u>Chapter 9</u>

How many Major Religions are there today?

From the following detailed list of major religions, we can easily determine the general category of non-believers in religion makes up only about 15.58% of the world's population. When you add in all the Buddhism followers, who also have no supreme God, then actual nonbelievers in God would make up a bit more than 22% of the world's population or 1.7 Billion people. This must seem to be a scary high number for the extreme evangelicals to digest!

For the world's organized religions, Christians make up about 31% of the population, Islam 24.8%, Hinduism 15.2%, Buddhism 6.6%, and Chinese combinations 5.6%. In total these 5 major religious groups make up most of the remaining 84% of the worlds total population. Therefore, if you are a nonbeliever you are definitely in the minority, that's assuming those professing to be religious are truly and devoutly religious!

<u>Religion Document</u>	<u># of Followers</u>		<u>Primary</u>
Christianity testament)	31.0%	2.382 Billion	The Bible (new
Islam	24.8%	1.907 billion	The Quran
Nonreligious	*15.58%*	*1.193 Billion*	
Hinduism Upanishads	15.2%	1.161 billion	The Vedas, The

Buddhism	**6.6%**	**506 Million**	The TIPITAKA, 40 volumes
Chinese	5.6%	394 Million	(Confucianism, Taoism combinations)
Ethnic Religions	3.0%	300 Million	
African	1.2%	100 Million	
Sikhism	.30%	26 Million	The Guru GRANTH Sahib
Spiritism	.2%	15 Million	
Judaism	.2%	14.7 Million	The Torah (1st 5 books of Hebrew Bible)
Baha'i	.07%	5.0 Million	
Jainism	.05%	4.2 Million	The Agamas
Shinto	.05%	4.0 Million	The KOJIKI
Cao Dai	.05%	4.0 Million	
Zoroastrianism	.03%	2.6 Million	The AVESTA
Tenrikyo	.02%	2.0 million	

The above list shows the major religious denominations and the percent of the world's population it supposedly represents. Within these main religious affiliations there are hundreds of sub divisions or minor variations of the primary religion. In the Christian religion alone there are Catholics, Protestant, Eastern Orthodox, Mormons and many more. To confuse the issue even further, each of those religions have further divisions such as within the Protestant group you have Anglican, Presbyterian, Lutheran, Baptist and the list continues to grow. Many times these sub groups are even further divided. Some scholars estimate today there are probably over 4,000 different religious variations in use around the world. Some of these 4,000 may vary only slightly by beliefs, location, language, or structure but they do vary. If you say you believe in a God, which one of the 4,000 religious variations do you think is actually the one true God or the real faith whose gospel you should faithfully follow?

Confusing doesn't properly describe the jumble of religious choices available from which to choose. Once you finally select one religion is it your duty to try to convince all of the other 3,999 variations yours is the only correct one to follow?

<u>Chapter 10</u>

Brief Descriptions of each Major Religion.

First let's define nonreligious people, who we usually call Atheist or Agnostic. This group of people currently make up a little over 15.59% or nearly 1.2 billion of the planet's population. As shown in the list in chapter 9, if you also add in all the Buddhism followers then actual nonbelievers in a supreme God would make up a bit more than 22% of the world's population or 1.7 Billion people. China has a population of around 1.4 billion people so if you add in many of those unknowns as probably being agnostic you could possibly get somewhere between 25 and 30 percent of the world as nonbelievers in any God. Apparently, it all depends on your worldview or your approach to life whether you tend to be religious or not. Everything affects your worldview including all your life experiences, relationships, teachings, and your understanding the nature of reality.

Nonbelievers just see the current human or the existing natural world and nothing beyond that. They do not believe there are at least two spaces where we could be present. However, religious people obviously believe there are at least two places for us to exist, one is the space where we actually spend our physical lives and the second place is such places as heaven or hell where your soul would finally end up. Most religions have these alternate unseen final locations and these places are called by many different names.

Basically, if you are not religious at all you must believe when you are dead you are completely gone from this physical world and that's the end; there is no alternate space for you, or your soul, or your spirit to ascend or descend into. Obviously for agnostics there is no such thing as a soul or other entities to worry about after you are dead. For these nonbelievers, death is the final end, and your existence is permanently completed. End of story!

For these nonbelievers what is the difference between being an Atheist or being an Agnostic? The short version is in an atheist's view they think the existence of God is highly improbable so they don't fully believe. An agnostic view is they know or believe for sure there is no such thing as a God.

An atheist believes you can not know for sure if there is a God so they choose to not to believe in any God. As said before, an agnostic believes fully and absolutely that there is no God! We all know others, who confess they are not sure if there is a true God, but they go through the process of faking their acceptance of one of the religions to hopefully stack the final deck in their favor; just in case.

We are now back to defining the religious people who actually do believe there is some mystical higher power. Obviously they believe in a supreme God or as is the case in some religions they believe in many Gods. They usually believe there are at least two spaces where we could exist. One is the physical space where we actually live our daily lives and the second is such fanciful places as heaven or hell where we go after we die.

Apparently some believe there is a third state of existence other than life itself and either heaven or hell and this third place is called purgatory. Purgatory is supposed to be where you go to wait for the final rapture, when God returns and judges whether you go up to heaven or down to hell. Note that Christians believe hell was created by God, ruled by God, and Satan is just an inmate of hell and not its ruler.

As previously stated, there are approximately 4,000 different subtle variations of religion but let's briefly explain the core beliefs of the top 5 religions. These are Christianity, Islam, Hinduism, Buddhism, and a grouping of Chinese beliefs such as Confucianism and Taoism.

Almost every religious text or spiritual book, such as the Bible or the Quran, have written passages open to some personal or scholastic interpretation or as some would put it "misinterpretation". This difference in interpretation of the sacred text usually creates some division within the main religion and sometimes these are extremely serious divisions. We all know of the wars fought between Catholics and Protestants who are Christians and more wars fought between Sunni and Shiite who are Muslim. The following will list the main arguments or theology for the religion's existence and obviously there is not room here to delve into the thousands of minor variations existing all around the world today.

Christianity

There are many variations within Christianity so it becomes a difficult task to narrowly define the religion itself. The over all premise states Jesus was the son of God and came to be born, suffered, and died so he could expunge all mankind's past sins and return people into God's good graces.

The Christian Bible has two main divisions, an old Testament and a new Testament. The old testament gospel was the original Hebrew Bible and presented almost the whole of traditional Jewish religion into Christianity. This old text was an extension of Judaism and is the stepping stone book leading up to the life of the promised one called Jesus, who was to be the saviour of all mankind. Jesus's life is depicted in the New Testament of the Bible and fulfills the prophecies from the old Jewish Hebrew Bible or the Old Testament. Jesus is supposed to be the son of God and the one sent by God to save all of us who believe in him.

The main prayer or **_Lords Prayer_** used by most Christian religions is basically the following with some minor text variation here and there.

- Our Father, which art in heaven,
- Hallowed be thy Name;
- Thy kingdom come;
- Thy will be done
- In earth, as it is in heaven:
- Give us this day our daily bread;
- And forgive us our trespasses,
- As we forgive them that trespass against us;
- And lead us not into temptation,
- But deliver us from evil;
- For thine is the kingdom,
- The power, and the glory.
- For ever and ever. Amen.

Any prayer, such as the one above from the Old Testament, is considered a spiritual practice allowing true believers to improve their relationship with their selected God. They may ask for his guidance to help solve a problem or just pray to find strength and solace in His presence.

The primary rules of the Christian faith are the original 10 commandments from the old testament. The followers of Christianity believe God wrote them down on a stone tablet for Moses to bring to the Hebrews and they must be followed if you want to enter heaven in the afterlife.

A condensed version of the **_10 Commandments_** follows:
1. You shall have no other gods before me.
2. You shall not make idols.
3. You shall not take the name of the LORD your God in vain.
4. Remember the Sabbath day, to keep it holy.
5. Honor your father and your mother.
6. You shall not murder.
7. You shall not commit adultery.
8. You shall not steal.
9. You shall not bear false witness against your neighbor.
10. You shall not covet (anything that is your neighbors).

Jesus explained the 10 Commandments and all of God's laws are based on Love and you must obey them to have eternal life. In Jesus teachings there were about 50 other rules for living a better life such as forgiving others, spreading the faith, and helping the disadvantaged. Jesus has said disobeying these laws and commandments shows a lack of love for God and our fellow humans and it causes suffering and broken relationships. God does not want anyone to live forever in a miserable state, causing suffering for themselves and others. Jesus said, "if you love me, keep my commandments".

The New Testament part of the Bible clearly states God's law is also a vital part of the New Covenant, the spiritual agreement God is making with Christians. Christians of today are still called to obey the original 10 Commandments as part of their love and loyalty to God.

Christians believe there will be a time in the future when God will bring on the "end" of the world. This eventual ending or "rapture" or God coming back to earth will be to uplift the true believers and to punish all those nonbelievers. In Christianity you can get redemption simply by asking forgiveness for all your sins even if you have done evil your whole life. Other religions believe you must do good for your entire life, or else!

Islam

Many people who are not Muslim are only aware of a few aspects of Islam. Many have only a slight passing knowledge about the Quran, Mecca, the 5 pillars of Islam and Sharia Law. Most non Muslims don't know believers in Islam also believe in previous revelations such as shown in the Jewish Torah, and Psalms, and the Gospel. Most of us are not aware Islam is supposed to be the final conclusion of the work started by earlier prophets and messengers such as Adam, Noah, Abraham, Moses, and also Jesus. Islam is supposed to be the complete and final version of all faith.

The Quran is the actual word of God himself and is verbatim and a final unaltered revelation as told to Muhammad directly by God through Gabriel. They believe Muhammad is the main and final prophet through whom their religion was completed. In summary, Muslims believe Muhammad is the last or final prophet who will ever be needed. The true religious path was started way back with Adam, Abraham, Moses, Jesus and is now finally completed by Muhammad. Muslims believe Jesus was only an important prophet, but not the promised messiah or the saviour of mankind as Christians believe.

The Quran is considered the most important holy book by Muslims and supersedes any previous writings. It does contain revelations and the sacred words given to Muhammad directly by God and also some older basic information found in the Hebrew Bible. Muhammad did not know how to write so his scribes wrote down his words as he dictated to them. The 114 chapters of teachings and examples of Muhammad provide a constitutional model for Muslims and were passed from Allah through Gabriel directly to Muhammad.

Islam states there is one incomparable God and there will be a final judgement where the righteous will be rewarded in paradise and the unrighteous will be punished in hell.

All Muslims must follow the *five basic pillars* and these are obligatory acts of worship and essential to the faith. These include:

1. to declare one's faith in God and belief in Muhammad
2. to prey 5 times a day (dawn, noon, afternoon, sunset, and evening)
3. to give to those in need
4. to fast during the month of Ramadan
5. to make a pilgrimage to Mecca, at least once if able to do so

Muslims must face toward Mecca when doing their daily prayers. Specific verses from the Quran are recited as an integral part of these daily prayers. Muslims must strive to maintain purity of mind, body, and soul during the prayer. They are seeking a deeper connection with Allah (God) and submitting to His will.

Islamic law, called Sharia law, touches on almost every aspect of Islamic life. These include banking and finance, men's and women's roles, welfare, and even the environment. It is fundamentally a faith based code of conduct showing all Muslims how they must live their daily lives. It dictates such things as how Muslims must modestly dress and outlines marriage and other moral principles. Pure Sharia law has exceedingly harsh punishments for transgressors but many Muslims do not support such ancient overly harsh punishments such as cutting off the hands of thieves.

At the beginning of the religion, around 610 CE, empire building was an essential part of the expansion of Islam as a religion. People loved the egalitarianism of the religion and flocked to be part of the new movement. There was a time when any opposition were required to accept Islam or die. Jews and Christians were assigned a special status as they were considered as being part of the community possessing scriptures like the Bible and were considered "people of the book". They were allowed religious autonomy but were required to pay a tax to retain their autonomy. The same status was later applied to the Zoroastrians from Persia and Hindus followers.

Hinduism
Unlike some of the other main religions this one has no specific founder who can be identified and it is considered to be the oldest religion in use today. Many see it as not a single religion but a combination of many philosophies and traditions involving different Gods and minor deities so it is often referred to as a "way of life" or a "family of religions". There are several different holy books and Hindus celebrate special symbols, and a wide variety of traditions, holidays, and customs. They worship "Brahman" who is a single deity but they also recognize other gods and goddesses. They believe in several

doctrines to please their God. One is *samsara* which is the continuous cycle of life, death, and reincarnation and the other is the much discussed *karma* which is the universal law of cause and effect or a general modern western term known as, "what goes around comes around".

Similar to other religions they believe in a soul but not just human souls but all living creatures have a soul. All these souls are part of the supreme soul and the end goal is to achieve salvation which ends the cycle of rebirths so you become part of the absolute soul. They believe your actions and thoughts directly determine your current life and also your future lives. Hindus strive to follow a code of living emphasizing good conduct and morality, so they can achieve the ultimate dharma. Hindus revere all living creatures so most practitioners of the religion will not eat beef or pork and many are vegetarians.

Hindu prayer is called Bhakti and is expressed through recitation of sacred songs, chants, and mantras. These devotional practices allow the person to deepen their connection with the divine. The end result is a higher sense of spiritual intimacy as well as a way to express their love, surrender, and reverence for the divine.

Buddhism,
Unlike other religions having a single deity or multiple deities, Buddhism has no God at the core of its

beliefs so it is non-theistic. Buddha was an actual person named Siddhartha Gautama who lived between 563-480 BCE in Nepal. Similar to today's world he was troubled by the sadness, anger, and violence he saw all around him and he felt he had to find a way to alleviate all this human suffering. After much study he finally spent 49 days in meditation and he reached an enlightened state and became Buddha. He traveled to many areas and spread the word until he died at age 80 and his teachings were recorded by monks who followed his travels. These teachings became the basis of the religion.

The core basis of the religion is to reach Nirvana or "a state beyond all suffering" which is the highest state and marks the end of human pain and suffering. It literally means "to blow out" or to "quench" the human cycle of death and rebirth or samsara until they find their way to liberation. He preached the way to Nirvana was mostly through dedicated meditation to build your own spiritual temple. Basically Buddha was a teacher and not a prophet or a God and he showed the way for others.

Buddha handed down what he called the *four Noble truths*:
1. All of human existence is suffering
2. The cause of suffering is craving
3. The end of suffering comes with putting an end to craving
4. There is a path we can follow to put an end to suffering

Buddha's suggested path to end suffering was to follow the *"Noble Eightfold Path"*.

1. *Right understanding*, there is a way to be free from suffering using 4 noble truths.
2. *Right thought,* engage in selflessness, altruism, and loving kindness in thoughts
3. *Right speech,* communicate in a way in line with compassionate thoughts without verbal abuse, lies, hatred or blame
4. *Right action,* abstain from murder, sexual misconduct, and theft
5. *Right livelihood,* engage in work that fulfills you and helps others. Avoid things that harm your body and mind, including drugs, alcohol, and other harmful substances.
6. *Right effort,* practice the noble eightfold path with consistency, not just on occasion or when it's easy.
7. *Right mindfulness,* observe the moving patterns of your body, mind, and the world around you without getting attached to your personal interpretation of these events.
8. *Right concentration,* regularly practice meditation that helps you observe what Buddhists call "the monkey mind". With the right concentration, your meditation practice will bring you even closer to the state beyond suffering.

The Buddhism religion or way of life does not believe in the eventual rapture or God coming back to earth to punish those nonbelievers. You get redemption and counter bad Karma by changing your ways, not just by asking forgiveness. You must strive to be a perfect human being, and in this way wise people create their own heaven, and if you don't these foolish people will create their own hell. Heaven or hell are just mental states of mind. There are no permanent or actual heaven or hell to go to for a Buddhist. It is especially important for a Buddhist to believe in humanity and each person is precious and important.

Meditation is central to Buddhist prayer practice. Various techniques and methods are employed to quiet the mind and develop inner awareness. This mindfulness meditation focuses on the present moment without any judgement with the intent to deepen one's own concentration and cultivate a deeper understanding of reality. Buddhists try to attain a state of tranquility, clarity, and insight through this meditation. Along with meditation Buddhists use sacred sounds or phrases as part of mantras and chanting to evoke specific qualities or states of mind. By Rhythmic chanting of scriptures or sutras they hope to generate positive energy and bring about a mental and spiritual transformation.

Chinese (Confucianism and Taoism),
Some history is in order here to be able to understand how religion exists in current day atheist China. China is a dictatorial Communist State and controls almost every aspect of life within the country, including how religion is to be viewed and tolerated. Some of the oldest religions or followings are appreciated as Chinese cultural heritage and are not subjected to strict rules like

"foreign" religions face. Communism in China took control in 1949 and today there has been a tightening of oversight of clergy and congregations to make sure all religion aligns with todays Chinese communism. Religions must be loyal to the party, and must somehow promote atheism. How any religion based on a supreme God can promote atheism, the western world has yet to figure out!

The recent blend of Marxism and Nationalism has tried to bring religion in line with traditional culture and atheist communism. The Chinese constitution states citizens enjoy "freedom of religious beliefs", however having said that, the government officially recognizes only 5 closely policed religions: Buddhism, Islam, Catholicism, Protestantism, and Taoism (Daoism).

There are 10 basic steps to describe how Communist China handles religion.

1. There is a policy of synchronization requiring all religious groups, especially foreign ones like Islam and Christianity, to align their doctrines, customs, and morality with Chinese culture and also show loyalty to the state.
2. Things must look more Chinese so crosses and minarets have been taken down from buildings. The clerics must focus on religious teachings to reflect on socialist values. There are plans to issue a more Chinese aligned Quran.
3. China has been accused of mass internment, surveillance, and torture of Muslim groups such as the

Uyghurs. The government has refuted these genocide accusations saying whatever they do is meant to improve Muslims lives and counter religious extremism.

4. Christians are officially allowed to worship in supervised official churches but many use private secret underground churches. The government has banned evangelization online and shutdown churches not officially registered. Some Christians and their leaders have been held in Chinese interment camps similar to the Muslim Uyghurs camps.

5. Han Buddhism is more leniently treated than Christianity or Islam. The government believes this branch of Buddhism has integrated former beliefs of Confucian, Daoist, and other traditional Chinese beliefs and customs. However, they have cracked down on Tibetan Buddhists to discourage loyalty to the exiled Dalai Lama.

6. China encouraged folk religion and ancient spiritual traditions because it considers them part of China's cultural heritage. China has allowed the veneration of the Chinese philosopher Confucius and is a great example of China's reverence for culture. The state supervises local folk religious activities to make sure they are guided by socialist values. If they don't conform they are eliminated and their buildings demolished.

7. If a religion falls outside of the 5 which are allowed or it does not meet a form of approved cultural heritage they are considered evil cults and are banned. Groups including Falun Gong, the Unification Church, and the Children of God are all considered cults and banned.

8. In general, the ruling Chinese Communist Party CCP promotes atheism and discourages religion. If you belong to the CCP you are banned from such spiritual activities except for rare engagement in cultural customs.

9. Children under 18 can not attend any religious affiliation so things like Sunday School and religious camps are prohibited. Schools must focus on promotion of non-religion and atheism and to join the communist youth party you must pledge a commitment to atheism.

10. Early in the communist revolution in 1949 their leaders denounced religion as "foreign cultural imperialism", "feudalism", and "superstition" and persecuted all religious groups. In 1968 Moa Zedong proceeded to have all old ideas, customs, and habits destroyed so unfortunately many churches, old shrines, temples, and mosques were eliminated.

With the ever present Chinese crackdown on global religions within China there still exists two local religious philosophies which are not considered anti-communist, these are Confucianism and Taoism.

Confucianism

There is a philosophy in China which was started over 2,500 years ago by a Chinese wise man called Confucius who lived between 551 and 479 BCE. He is considered China's most famous philosopher, teacher, and political theorist and he has interjected profound influence in China and many other Asian countries.

Chinese Confucianism is a combined worldview, a social ethic, a political ideology, a scholarly tradition, and a way of life which has lasted for well over 2,000 years. It is not an organized religion in the true sense but more of a philosophy and a way of life emphasizing ethical values for human interactions between people, communities, and nations. Many people belonging to other organized religions still call themselves Confucians because of their daily philosophy of life which does not conflict with their religious beliefs.

The Chinese Communist government tolerates this Confucian thinking as long as it does not interfere with their socialist values and because they consider it as part of Chinese culture to be preserved for future generations.

An example of Confucius thought was when he was asked whether a person's worth should be measured by their ability and strength of character and should those born into privilege have it stripped from them until they prove themselves worthy. His answer was he wanted to change the old standard rules so they would now favour the virtuous and competent. He believed a few good men of integrity could effect the fate of the many. But these good men had to be tested in their politics to be better prepared with knowledge and skills to serve their rulers properly and to prove their worth through their own moral influence.

Confucius felt, simply being brave and loyal was" hardly the way to be good", because if you didn't have the advantage of thought and love for learning, people would not be able to know whether their judgement had been misguided or whether their actions might lead them and others down a perilous path to maybe a violent end.

Taoism: (Daoism)

Taoism is both a religion and a philosophy from ancient China connected to writings by a philosopher Lao Tzu from around 500 BCE. The main premise is both humans and animals should live in balance with the universe or the TAO. The emphasis is focused on observance of natural cosmic forces or "going with the flow" which they think flows through all things and binds or releases them. The religion portion developed out of their belief in cosmic balance maintained and regulated by the Tao but todays version has evolved to include ancestor and spirit worship.

The Tao main document is the TAO-TE-CHING. It is not a scripture as we understand them but is a book of poetry showing the simple way of following the Tao so you live a life at peace with one's self, with others, and with the changing world. Don't fight against life, just yield to circumstance and let unimportant things just go. Empty your pride so you are open to learning from other people and don't insist you are right all the time. Bend to new ideas and new ways of living and don't cling to old belief patterns and the past.

As far as a heaven or an afterlife is concerned none existed for Taoism. The afterlife only existed in the current life you were living. You were always eternally within your essence.

That was a brief look at the 5 top religions of the world. As noted there are hundreds of off-shoots to consider so if you want to investigate all the variations within each religion; good luck with that!

Chapter 11

What actually rules your life if you are not religious:

One obvious question is "can a nonbeliever in any God assume various parts of each religion and end up a perfectly good person without actually being part of any specific organized religion"? Of course they can! What steps could you do to succeed at this task?

- First, let's adopt the last 6 of the 10 commandments and you follow all those, it just makes common sense as most of them are usually part of the established laws of the land anyway or are at least the current social convention.

- You can always revere the earthly environment around you like First Nations, Islam, and Hinduism preach because we are all dead if you don't look after the environment.

- You must be careful of what activities you do so bad *karma,* which is the universal law of cause and effect, will not affect you even if you don't really believe in karma.

- For your own long term physical health, you can keep your body pure and not smoke, drink alcohol, or do drugs like Buddha said.

- You can meditate like Buddha to calm your mind and appreciate all the simple things in life.

- You can give directly to the poor and do other charitable activities just as most religions preach.

- You can yield to circumstance and let unimportant things go and bend to new ideas like in Chinese Tao.
- You can revere your parents and ancestors like Confucians.
- You can be like Buddhists and try to attain a state of tranquility, clarity, and insight through thoughtful meditation.
- You can be courteous, loving, and kind to everyone like Christians preach.
- You can enjoy the music of the faithful at holiday time and enjoy the cuisine and festivals from many different cultures.
- Above all else you can be respectful of all religions and never take their God's name in vain, so you don't offend the faithful.

You will have noticed in the above list there is no mention of having a faith in any supreme being or all powerful God. Heaven and hell do not enter into the agnostic picture and there is no mention of a soul.

None of the listed life choices are particularly difficult to follow and can lead to a full and enjoyable life without believing in any supreme God or specific religion. That's the author's take on all of the major religions. Logically you just pick and choose from the various religions and follow the best humanitarian parts; plain and simple is it not? You don't give financial donations to God or to a church, you give directly to the needy instead.

The big kicker here is the one not mentioned yet. What about when you die? Is it a necessity that you supposedly end up in some magical wonderful place for eternity or was actually living one stressful life simply sufficient for you? Believing in No God means in death you just end your existence and maybe that's finally enough for most people!

What about someone who was the perfect citizen and a great humanitarian for all of his life but did not believe in a God. If there really is a heaven would a merciful God say to him "well your screwed and off to hell you go"! Going to hell in this specific instance doesn't seem particularly fair or justified now does it?

Death: (the final cessation of all life processes)
One of the big inconsistencies about our human existence is our obvious fascination with our death! A strange conundrum to say the least. As we live our day to day life many of us constantly worry about death, especially as we age. Religious people seem to be so worried about where we might go after we die it becomes a constant annoying presence in their daily life. Muslims having to prey 5 times a day is a great example of this daily religious intrusion. The only absolute certainty from the day you are born is that someday you will die, so why should we be so preoccupied with the prospect; it's going to happen to all of us eventually.

When someone we know dies we go to the archaic ritual called a funeral. Here we proclaim we are celebrating the dead person's life. Seems to be a bit too late to do that, would it not have been better to celebrate the person while they were still living and not wait till they were dead?

Regarding death, there seems to be two major issues we carry around for most of our adult life. We might worry where will we end up after we die, heaven or hell, but for many of us the main worry is how we will die and not the dying itself. No one wants to suffer for many years just waiting for the inevitable end. It would be assumed a quick sudden death would be preferred by most people.

We won't go into all the ramifications of when you are actually considered biologically dead. Is it when both brain and heart stop functioning or when the brain stops functioning but what if the heart still beats? We will leave that determination up to the professors, doctors, and lawyers to figure it all out.

If you are overly religious does that mean you are obsessed with where you might end up for eternity. It would seem to some, living for eternity would be exceptionally boring after a few centuries, would it not! If on the other hand if you are an agnostic, you don't have this afterlife to worry about because there is no more existence in any form once you are dead. When you are dead that's it, you are permanently gone, and that's the end of you, period.

Along with the previous conundrum about dying, religious people have the perplexing issue of when can a terminally ill person legally or morally take his own life or have someone help them if unable to do the act themselves. These final determinations are labeled euthanasia and physician-assisted suicide. Most all of our religions firmly state it is morally wrong to take a life including your own! They believe God granted us life and only he can take it away, even to end the suffering of the sick patient. We are told we must let life take its course because that was God's plan. Maybe suicide was really in God's plan for you if you believe he plans everything, who actually knows! But what if you are a nonbeliever and there is no so called "God's plan" for your entire existence, it should be acceptable to end your own life should it not?

All religions also state that the patient may refuse extraordinary measures to extend life if they desire no help to prolong their existence. Keep in mind that all these religions also believe there is a soul attached to the body so death is an important part of going into the afterlife. However, you are definitely not allowed to hasten the trip to the religious afterlife by committing suicide. There is no formal Hindu statement on this suicide issue but it would negatively affect the person's karma for the next life so it is probably not a good idea.

Many physicians believe there is a natural dying process that starts about 3 months before actual death. This would normally be older people whose system is beginning to shut down and will stop functioning completely in from 4 to 12 weeks. This body shutting down process varies greatly depending on the person's age and their physical health attributes. Apparently at some point our physical body will have run its course and your time is up. You can prolong it somewhat but can not stop it no matter how hard you try!

There are specific symptoms that indicate the dying process has begun. Signs such as reduced thirst and appetite, increased need for sleep, loss of weight and an unusual sense of calm. During the last couple of weeks of life there are more serious medical indicators such as lower body temperature and blood pressure, increased sweating, unusual pulse, breathing issues, and a lack of verbal communication. These are the recognized natural signs of an end of life. Some surviving relatives might simply state "the person just gave up" but more likely it was the physical body actually reaching its normal end of life and the person had no tangible decision in the matter. The warrantee on their physical body had finally expired!

Now many might ask, if there is no soul or spirit how do we explain the many thrilling TV shows showing intensive investigations of haunted houses and obvious signs of what they perceive as paranormal activity. We are told these are probably wondering souls looking for the way to leave the earth!

First let's state that all these types of reality shows are notorious for exaggerating the situation and in some cases actually staging the supposed apparition simply to gain TV audience. Now I personally do not have any exposure to such paranormal happenings but my niece who is a nurse has experienced one such event. She worked in a large facility that looked after seniors and was located in what was formerly a large multiple story school building. In this school two children had died in a swimming pool accident many years before. The ghosts of these two kids apparently liked to perform practical jokes on the staff such as making the empty elevator go up and down or hiding their desk pen. When the working adults in the long term care home told the kid's ghosts to knock it off the kids seemingly obeyed. Was this simply some people pulling off practical jokes or some other explainable occurrence? What was the real explanation for this supposed ghostly activity, your guess is as good as mine? The practical joker theory seems the most logical!

Chapter 12

Why we may not believe in God!

There are probably many reasons why someone would not believe in a God, but here are a few of the more obvious:

1. You are a personality type who does not want to give up any control
2. Hard to believe in something you can't see, but wants to run your life
3. Science seems to refute much of the creationist parts of the Bible
4. Too many religious choices, which one is the real one to follow
5. Terrible experiences with other supposed religious people
6. Hard to believe in a religious book written long after the events occurred
7. Many think religious people are missing something others have
8. God seems to have too many different temperaments

Reason one:

All religions which are based on creator gods means a God ends up having the ultimate authority over you and strips us of our individuality and freedom. So if you are a so called "control freak" type of personality you may not like to give up that much control. Many with this personality do not like to sit in a pew of a church because they feel trapped, so they give up on religion altogether. People such as these do not feel in control when their freedom of movement is controlled by other circumstances, such as sitting through a long speech of even attending a sports event where their free movement is somewhat limited. They usually have a domineering type of personality and do not want to feel dominated or controlled by something else like a God they can not hear or see. They also question how can Christians have free will if God already has a plan for everyone. This concept of a predetermined controlled life by God is just to far fetched for "control freak" personalities and most other nonbelievers to accept.

Reason two:

Some people are just too pragmatic and find it impossible to believe in something all powerful but remains invisible. These people tend to be the type who would insist "show me" before they will agree to anything. Nonbelievers have a difficult time believing in an unseen entity such as a soul. Without a soul then the concept of heaven is an impossibility. The idea of hell, where one is expected to spend eternity suffering, seemingly goes against the idea of a merciful God. Educated people find the idea of any supreme God a difficult concept to accept. The thought of a supreme being actually creating the massive universe and controlling or having a plan for every aspect of life within it is just too preposterous for them to grasp. These nonbelievers also do not fall for dumb ridiculous conspiracy theories and can easily determine the difference between facts and fiction.

Reason three:

Modern science has pretty much determined humans evolved over a couple million years and were not created in one magical day. Similarly, we now have a good idea how the planets and stars were formed over billions of years, not in 6 days. These scientific truths seem to put a pretty big hole in the biblical creationist stories leading to further doubts about the other religious stories in the Bible. Nonbelievers have a difficult time believing in unnatural miracles when modern day science using physics and biological evidence explains much about how our natural world functions. With these obvious biblical creation flaws can a science believer and creationist doubter actually believe what it says in the rest of the Bible?

Reason four:

There are scores of main religions and countless offshoots out there, nonbelievers think an all powerful God would have fixated on the correct one and easily eliminated the imposters. Nonbelievers are sure if there was a God he would have backed the correct religion and done away with all the imposters thus eliminating all ambiguity. Even similar religions can't agree amongst themselves as to which is the "right" one, so how are we nonreligious examiners supposed to figure it all out? Blind faith is one thing; outright logic is another!

Reason five:

Many of us have known people who profess to be ultra religious and they eventually act as the worst kind of human being. This phony pretense tends to put us off at least their form of religion. The various sex scandals and other misbehaving of supposed religious leaders can scar you for life and keep you from going back into their church or indeed any church. Religions trying to keep women subjugated and repressed based on outdated religious texts and only seeing them as second class citizens and not as equals is another off-putting religious practice for many.

Reason six:

Many of the oldest religions have a religious text we are to follow, but most of these texts were compiled by ordinary men many years after the original event took place. For us to believe the text is now the word of God when we know it was created by humans who have their own inherent biases is a bit of a stretch for some doubters. Nonbelievers are convinced that the Bible is an old record that has been translated from Hebrew, Aramaic, and Greek by many men who obviously were influenced by their own biases, preconceptions, and possible prejudicial directions from superiors. These and other very human traits would naturally be a major influence in what they chose to write down for us to follow. Even the current actual Christian bible has several versions, over 30 variations so far. Nonbelievers have a problem when they see Christians only choosing to follow some of what was written in the Bible and reject other passages. They reject what is said in the Bible and now accept homosexuality and mixed fabrics but at present time they reject stoning as a punishment.

Reason seven:

Some think to be a diehard believer in a religion you have to be missing something in your own mental makeup. This gap is only filled by believing in an unseen mystical being. These people are mentally stable otherwise, what is this missing piece of their makeup is not clear? Somehow they don't feel fulfilled without some kind of religion in their life. The rest of us feel fulfilled and normal without religion so we don't get the attraction or feel the need for religion some others obviously feel.

Reason eight:

The Christian God is supposed to be a loving God so why does he allow so much pain, cruelty, and needless suffering especially when one human does it to another human. Why are wars, atrocities, and natural disasters allowed to inflict such misery on mankind? Would not a merciful God have prevented his followers from committing genocide and racism against a weaker society. Why was Jesus put through such barbaric torture to die so horribly, could not God have just forgiven humanity directly? How can a God be both just and merciful but at the same time be jealous and demanding?

In summary, if you can't see God, can't fully believe in the religious texts, don't like your past exposure to religious people or their leaders, don't want to give up control over your own life, and are happy and fulfilled, why would you follow an unseen God with seemingly confusing personalities. Many believe if there really was a God he would not allow so much pain and suffering in our world to occur. There are obviously many more reasons why someone would be a nonbeliever but these seem to be the major issues most nonbelievers will most likely be concerned with. Pure faith versus pure logic seem to be the main overriding topic shown here.

Chapter 13

The Main Religious Divides:

The specific beliefs in such things as an afterlife, a soul, a spirit, or angels is another way religions each show their uniqueness as well as their similarities.

Afterlife:

As far as an afterlife is concerned, religions can be quickly divided down into two divergent groups. One group believes there is a creator God who created everything and followers can miraculously be saved if they simply ask for forgiveness. In the final end of the world or "rapture", this God will appear on earth and destroy the wicked unsaved people, and protect the good religious' believers. This group of religions which are offering last minute forgiveness would be Christianity, Islam, and others. The saved souls will supposedly go onto everlasting life in heaven while those not saved will go to never ending punishment in hell.

The second religious group does not believe in what group one believes but instead they strive for redemption by changing their current everyday ways and to always do good. Their followers must recognize and follow moral and spiritual values throughout their entire life. Just asking for forgiveness at the end of life is not good enough for these religions.

All religions based on a creator god means God ends up having ultimate authority over us humans and strips us of our individuality and freedom. Therefore, you must be a devotee of a specific religion to obtain salvation even if you have been a perfectly righteous individual in every other way. You could even be a sinful person for all of your life but if you finally ask for forgiveness you can still end up in heaven. Buddhists do not believe in this last minute forgiveness theory and demand you must be virtuous for all of your life. They also believe all people should show respect and especially tolerance to everyone regardless of their religious following.

The great divide between religions is between asking for forgiveness at the end of life or being righteous all the days of your life, not just at the end. Apparently an afterlife is not as straight forward and simple as it seems and there are other major religious divisions as well.

Soul:

One other religious divide is the question "do you have a soul which passes onto another dimension such as heaven or hell after death or does your soul remain as part of a larger entity here on earth"? The real question should be, "do you even have this magical entity called a soul". It is also unseen like God is unseen, so naturally we have to question does a soul actually exist? If every living thing has a soul, what was or is the soul's purpose?

What exactly is your soul supposed to be? Britannica defines a "soul, in religion and philosophy, as the immaterial aspect or essence of a human being, that which confers individuality and humanity, often considered to be synonymous with mind or the self. In theology, the soul is further defined as the separate part of the individual which partakes of divinity and often is considered to survive the death of the body".

Many cultures believe humans have this entity called a soul and some religions actually believe everything living thing has a soul. Each religion develops its own theory about the soul's origin, mortality, and relationship to the body. Some old religions like those found in ancient Egypt and Greece actually believed humans had two or more souls representing different aspects of life.

For all of mankind's existence there has been much theoretical discussion about what is a soul and how does it attach itself to each human. For most religions to work effectively or work at all, there must be a soul present in each of us to provide the desired end result after death of the physical body, which is for your soul to end up in heaven. Without a soul it would seem there is no possible life after death! In reality, without a soul or something similar, there is no reason for most religions to exist.

Spirits:

The term "spirit" apparently is another word taking on different meaning depending on each religion. Even the old and new testament define it slightly different. It basically refers to God or a version of God and has nothing to do with a person's soul or the specific individual themselves.

Angels:

Angels are mentioned in almost every culture throughout history. Basically angels seem to be a conduit between humans and their unseen Gods. Here again each religion has created their own version of angels with specific attributes and tasks.

Some believe there are guardian angels or spiritual entities who protect and guide an individual person or an entire group or even an entire nation. Many believe that God does not communicate with us directly but He may use angels to communicate with us instead but in quiet subtle methods such as in dreams, intuition, signs, or visions.

Most of our primitive or indigenous societies also have had these invisible angel beings existing between the real world and the spirit world. These unseen angels acted as a kind of special messenger between people or animals and a higher power. Many people and some entire cultures believe each person has their own guardian spirit or angel.

Hindus believe there are angels who act only as spiritual communicators with people. Buddhists have angles they call Devas and are souls who have been reincarnated into a higher spiritual plane and can only be seen by those who have been spiritually awakened.

As far back as our recorded history goes there is mention of afterlife, souls, spirits, and angels. Does this mean today we are simply perpetuating these old ancient superstitious myths? These myths have been carried forward from uneducated early humans who dreamed up these things to justify or clarify what they perceived as unexplainable happenings.

You have never actually seen God. You have never in fact seen your soul or any soul. You have never truly communicated with an angle. You have never communicated with someone who has passed away! Does this all mean these are actually just old myths carried forward to justify their form of religion. Seems like these are all just myths to most current day agnostics.

Chapter 14

What Does Science say about Some Religious Beliefs?

How was the planet we live on actually constructed and how were we humans and other earthly creatures created; science has one answer and all old religions have another.

Biblical Theory:

Using only the Bible as a timeline guide, religious scholars have determined the planet was created about 9,000 years ago by God in only six, 24 hour long days. It states God created the world and everything we see in the universe out of what you couldn't see, or out of nothing.

- Day 1 – light and time
- Day 2 – the sky and "separated waters"
- Day 3 – dry ground, bodies of water, and plants
- Day 4 – the sun, moon, stars, and planets
- Day 5 – fish and birds
- Day 6 – land animals and humans
- Day 7 – he rested from his work

God supposedly did this masterful creation of our beautiful planet to show us how he loved us. To this end he put together the perfect world for us to live and rule over. This utopian world apparently ended when Adam and Eve succumbed to sinful temptation and screwed the whole thing up.

That's a brief explanation of how everything came to be, based on several accounts from the most popular religions. You can read thousands of religious papers from various religions explaining in detail what each day of creation was all about and what it meant based on their own unique interpretation. The Biblical and other creation descriptions and its intended detail meaning all depends on which religion's perspective from which you obtain your information.

Evolution Theory:
Now a detailed scientific explanation on how the planet and human life evolved would also fill volumes of texts to explain every detail. There is a huge amount of scientific information just on how a single cell evolved and slowly changed to be able to combine with other cells to form much more complicated multi cell structures, such as humans. Considerable more detail is also available on things like RNA and DNA and more is being discovered all the time. How we humans evolved over the millennia from a single cell located in the world's oceans to a walking talking individual is another extremely long complicated trek through biology.

If we take a quick trip specifically through cell investigation and list a few of the massive terminology used today it might give you a small sense of the enormity of the overall field of cell study. Terms such as the following: Enzyme, membrane, ribosomes, genetic code, nucleotides, codon, amino acid, eukaryotic cell, cytoskeleton, cell-to-cell communication, endocytosis, vacuoles, mitochondrion, and chloroplast are a short list of a few of the many terms scientists use within this complicated field of cell study. This scientific study is only one of countless areas of complex research dedicated to unravelling the mysteries of how we evolved over several million years from single cells into the current human form. We can actually see some minor evolutionary change ourselves by just observing how much taller we humans are today than even a couple generations ago.

Science shows how mankind evolved through several different stages over the last million or so years to eventually be todays Homo Sapiens. Our most recent walking upright species probably evolved only about 315,000 years ago. Apparently there were similar species before us as there is fossil evidence going back well over a million years. These recently uncovered human fossils show there were a couple different early members of our Humanoid group or human like tribe of ancestors actually predating our current group.

We apparently lived at the same time as another now extinct tribe called the Neanderthals. Some scientists are convinced we originated from a long extinct member of the ape family as Darwin argumentatively hypothesized. There is enough evidence collected from several areas of recent study to convince modern day scientists our ancestors interacted with other distinct groups of now extinct humanoids as they traveled out of their original home lands in Africa or Asia. If we look objectively at the fossil record, the genetic evidence, and the archeological findings we will notice we current humans have much more in common with these other now extinct versions of ourselves than we previously thought.

As far as how the planet itself evolved, the short version is it all supposedly started about 13.5 billion years ago when the enormously concentrated mass of matter suddenly and rapidly expanded (not exploded) sending huge amounts of material out into an empty universe. Recent studies suggest that the universe might be at least twice that age or 26 billion years old. The more precise our space travelling telescopes get, the further back in time we can seemingly observe, the more we discover about the origin and timing of the current universe.

During the Big Bang many types of matter were supposedly formed in the first trillionth of a second. As all this matter quickly moved outward some of it began to collect together and transformed over billions of years to end up becoming stars, planets, clouds of gasses, and other space material. Using this original space matter as a start, we can still see new stars and their planets are actually continuing to collect and develop out in the vastness of space. All this space material is still moving outward from the spot of the original "big bang". In fact, recent study seems to show the rate of outward expansion has even sped up ever so slightly, a very puzzling fact to be sure.

About 9 billion years after the big bang or around 4.5 billion years ago our sun and the rest of the solar system formed from one of the rotating clouds of gas and dust originally ejected out into space during the big bang. This spinning solar nebula of loose material eventually spun faster and faster until its growing gravity flattened into a gigantic disk. Most of the material was pulled inward by intense gravity towards the newly forming sun at the center of the disk. The remaining debris, further away from the powerful gravitational pull of the sun, collected and formed the individual planets and are continuing to revolve around the center of the Solar System.

The sun is what gives us heat, light, seasons, weather, and life on our planet. It is driven by massive nuclear fusion reactions; these are not to be confused with our manmade fission reactions like our atom bombs.

Fusion reactions, like what happens on the sun, are naturally occurring and fission reactions are only manmade. To generate the same energy our sun produces every second we would have to explode about 100 billion tons of dynamite. The Sun is indeed a powerful force and without it we perish!

To explain the gigantic scale of the universe you must understand our Sun is just one of more than an estimated 400 billion stars in our Milky Way galaxy and our Sun is only a minor star. It has been proven many of these other stars also have one or more planets circling around them just as our sun. This is a truly amazing number of stars and planets in just our galaxy but our Milky Way Galaxy is just one galaxy of an estimated one trillion other galaxies existing out there in space. The size of the entire vast universe and the quantity of stars identified so far is so large it is almost incalculable for us minor mortals to fully comprehend. One would logically have to ask, if God created everything why bother creating trillions of other stars and billions more planets?

How the sun actually functions is also a miraculous wonder, but it is explainable. It has enough fuel to last for about 5 billion more years before it burns out. Like other stars it is made up of mostly Hydrogen and a lesser amount of Helium as well as oxygen, carbon, neon, nitrogen, magnesium, iron and silicon. The suns core has such high pressure and temperatures around 15 million degrees Celsius that it's gravity compresses Hydrogen so tight their atoms fuse together creating helium in a reaction process called nuclear fusion. The end result of this chain reaction compression is the sun gives off tremendous amounts of energy we experience mostly in the form of visible light, plus invisible infrared, and ultraviolet parts of the electromagnetic spectrum.

The above is an overly simplified explanation of the accepted modern scientific version of how planets and humans were created, it is quite a different story from the 6 days of creation as stated in the Bible. These two theories ultimately create the division between how science and religion try to explain how we and the planet eventually arrived to the form and appearance existing today.

An interesting side note here is all matter found in the universe is believed to have been first created by the big bang and scattered way out into space. We humans, who are made up of carbon and other common space elements, are actually made of the same original space material as all of the stars we see in the beautiful night sky. This all means we humans are ultimately made from this same star material as well.

Since we are talking about the wonders of star creation and their material makeup, think of humanities expertise in the current time frame and compare it to a thousand years ago. Long ago we humans had to dream up Gods to explain the mysteries of creation of the stars and of course us humans. Now consider a modern day example. We humans have retrieved a sample of material from and asteroid that was two hundred million miles away from earth. This asteroid we visited was in a much larger elliptical orbit than our planet and was moving at an incredible speed. Think about the complicated math involved to launch a rocket from Earth and hit such a small fast moving target so far away.

It took this Japanese space craft about 3.5 years to travel the vast distance to the one-kilometer wide spinning rock asteroid, actually land on it, mechanically collect a sample of material, and launch from it to return to earth. In total the space craft traveled 3.25 billion miles over 6 years. That unmanned exploration trip is truly amazing when you think of all the new technical machinery created and the massive amount of calculations involved regarding weight, speed, thrust, gravity, direction, and distance. Now was God responsible for all of this activity, was it his plan as some may think, or was it just us?

Now if we humans are smart enough to accomplish this majestic roundtrip space voyage to a far off asteroid why can't we solve the global warming problem before it kills us all? Whether you believe in God or not, I doubt He would want us to destroy our own beautiful blue planet!

Chapter 15

Evolutionary Theory or Intelligent Design:

Examining modern day biology and olden day theology we obviously have two distinct theories about where mankind originated. As described above, one theory is science based on evolution and the other theory is based on a faith that a God created us.

If one is to believe in _evolutionary theory,_ where we just came into being by evolving over a few million years, there doesn't seem to be a need for an all-powerful creator to have put us on the planet. We evolved into our current form just like how everything else evolved on the planet, including the planet itself. We now know the chemical building blocks of life and a great deal of how DNA (deoxyribonucleic acid) works. We have deciphered much of the DNA double helix structure and are beginning to use this knowledge to do some miraculous medical procedures. We know all organisms are built from the same six essential ingredients: carbon, hydrogen, nitrogen, oxygen, phosphorus and sulfur all of which are plentiful on our planet.

This field of evolutionary biology has much proof in the form of human like fossils found in many parts of the world spanning at least two million years of human history. These fossils show a discernable evolution to prove we actually evolved over a couple million years to the point where we are today. You can actually believe in this scientific evolution theory and still believe in an all-powerful God, and many of the world's best and brightest scientists do actually believe in both.

To believe in the other _creationist or intelligent design_ approach you have to put aside all evolution science and firmly believe in a creator or God. You know the one where "God created man in one day in his image". We sceptics always have to ask "in what God image, a short black man from Ethiopia or a tall Tutsi warrior type from central Africa". This question always sparks a rebuttal, especially from a white evangelical Christian. Also, people who are against racism always like to remind the diehard white Christian racists, Jesus was also a Jew. This simple statement of fact frequently seems to stop them dead in their tracks because these racists can't logically think, reason, or accept Jesus was born a Jew.

We wonder did some fictional God play a part in all the major astrological episodes over the past 4.5 billion years eventually creating us and our planet? Could it not have simply been the normal progression of chemistry, physics, and biology naturally proceeding throughout the development of our entire universe and of course us? Most of us will remain entrenched in either the evolutionary theory which took four billion years or the intelligent design all done in six-days theory, and most will never be convinced to change beliefs. That's unfortunate because you can pretty much prove the science evolution theory but there is no physical proof at all of the intelligent design, religion oriented theory.

Chapter 16

What Did Religions Influence:

Most people rightly acknowledge religion has had a huge influence on many things we experience everyday. Such varied topics as war, government structure, laws and legal punishments, culture, human rights, morals, dress codes, art, music, architecture, and racism. All of these topics have been strongly affected and influenced by religions over the past couple thousand years. But does simply admitting to these magnificent past influences of religion justify continuing on with religion in a modern day society? Conversely can we say "thank you for this great start", now we will carry on without needing any constant interaction from any religion!

Would all these topics have progressed to their current form without our past exposure and influences from organized religions, probably not! But now mankind seems to have universally adopted these mostly social influences and they are now propagated without needing worldly religions being imposed on them any further. Knowing all this we therefore must ask "should religions continue to exist"? Can we say definitively these various topics or influences are now so well ingrained in our cultures they will carry on even without organized religions as a durable guide, agnostics think they can?

War Influence:

We have had wars called "Holy Wars" and "Wars of Religion" but most often religion did not play the most important part in causing the conflict in the first place. The obvious exception were the crusades where Christians wanted to drive out the Muslims from Jerusalem and of course the European wars being fought between the Catholics and Protestants. The fighting between the Muslims and Hindus after India obtained its independence from Great Britain was not a war as we usually consider it but the bloody civil unrest was deadly for many and was religiously based to be sure.

European religious wars were most obvious in the 1500's and 1600's from the French internal wars from 1562-1598 and the so called thirty year wars 1616 to 1648 and the English Civil War ending in 1651. There have been times when French Catholics joined with German Protestants against another Catholic French king. There have been Catholic rulers fighting another Catholic ruler with Islamic assistance, we can see there have been some strange alliances during all of these so called Wars of Religion. Sometimes even the Pope would go to war against another monarch who was also a Catholic such as Philip 2nd of Spain. We can observe that historically sometimes a religion was a war's cause but it was not the usual primary factor in most wars. Most often wars were fermented by territorial encroachment, social or racial anxieties, political expansionism, or simple plain economic grievances.

It would seem recently the most "war like" religion would be Islam, although past European Christian history such as the world wars started in 1914 and 1939 might disprove the analogy completely. Warfare in the Islamic religion has been an integral part of spreading or protecting the faith since Muhammad was around. Jihad or "to struggle in the way of God by the sword" is a war concept linking the political and religious justification for war for those extreme purists in the Islamic religion.

Hinduism does not have any history of worldwide warfare at least on purely religious grounds; perhaps if you want to be religious and avoid warfare this is the one faith to chose.

Wars between entire civilizations were not as common as conflicts within a given civilization such as we saw in India in the late 1940s. Sometimes these conflicts are religious wars but most often they were caused by other factors. If you consider all of Europe a civilization, you can understand this constant war analogy. Internal conflicts inside China is another great example of wars repeatedly carried on within a given civilization. We can see some wars were religion oriented but most were not!

Government structure Influence:

Many times governments and religion are extensively intertwined right from the outset. Centuries ago religion was used to create a structure for citizens to follow and this enforced a new standard social order, this structure eventually evolved and became the entrenched form of government. During these ancient civilizations there was actually no divide between religious authority and political authority because of the high degree of integration between the two. Most civilizations evolved and separated the two authorities, religion and government, but many have not! Iran and Afghanistan are two extreme examples of nations where religion and government are essentially the same thing.

The Bible states Jesus said "Give to Caesar what is Caesar's and give to God what is God's." in other words you must pay your taxes. The Bible also says you must obey the laws and pay taxes for two reasons, one so you are not punished, and two because you know you should. Also government workers need to be paid so they can keep doing God's work, and their work is serving you. This Christian religious tax analogy definitely flies in the face of current republican philosophy who are so adamantly anti tax, yet proclaim to be so religious. This is another typical republican two-faced hypocrisy showing they are not purely following their much touted stance on evangelical religion as they always claim.

In today's governments most secular orientated citizens want a definite separation of church and state. This separation means all citizens are free to practice whatever religion they want or no religion at all if they so choose. Most importantly, all faiths are free from any government interference. However, this seems not to be the case in China or in Islamic ruled nations where Islamic law and normal government laws sometime differ. In the western world, Muslims are supposed to follow the laws of the countries where they reside but they are also subjected to problems if the country's foreign policy takes actions which would be against their own religious based Islamic Laws. This dichotomy of laws and religion makes some Muslim citizens confused as to the correct course to follow.

Laws and legal punishments Influence:

Going back in time it is difficult to establish whether religion had much influence on the legal apparatus of the oldest societies. We would have to assume any government laws put into force back in those days could not be in conflict with the established and all powerful religion of the day. Even the Bible's Ten Commandments established essential rules to be followed but did not layout any specific "legal" punishments for the transgressors.

Many of us remember the old biblical saying of "an eye for an eye" and wrongly assume the old laws were extremely brutal. It actually was meant to express the principle regarding the punishment for law breakers and as such the punishment should only be equal to the harm the illegal action had caused. In Hebrew it meant "an eye in place of an eye" so any punishment was to just mirror the actual offence and not be worse than the original crime. It was to reduce the vengeful retribution some victims sought as punishment. The saying actually predates the Hebrew bible because it has been found in Babylonian legal code called the Code of Hammurabi and it is there to show the penalty for an injustice should only match the severity of the crime and limit any compensation to the value of the actual loss. This harsh sounding phrase of an eye for an eye was actually more about maintaining order and attempting to prevent excessive vengeance. Whether the Babylonian religion of the time influenced this logical application of law is unknown but it has been presented in further religions and was usually accepted by the legal authorities of the era.

Similar to the eye for an eye approach, the Jewish Torah says you cannot compensate for a death so there should only be a monetary solution. Obviously todays nonreligious legal systems, which are present in many nations, take a much different approach and utilize the death penalty for the guilty as the final punishment. This has become more of a social approach and not a strictly religious approach to punishment! Iran had executed over

850 people in 2023 which was an eight year high and is much higher than America's 23 executions for the same year. Most civilized nations (145 out of 200) no longer use the death penalty as punishment.

Originally a civilization's laws were often indistinguishable from the norms of the prevalent religion of the day. The blended civilian and religious laws usually carried harsh punishments as they broke both the norms of the religion as well as society's laws. Once the punishment was completed the person had his guilt fully discharged and they could return to society. Todays punishments are meant more to prevent further harm and not so much as to purify the soul of the guilty party. Some would suggest a certain amount of vengeance should be applied to a sentence and it is sometimes hard to determine if a punishment is strictly to prevent further harm or has it had a tinge of vengeance added.

Modern day law is often referred to as positive law and it evolved and was formalized from the early religious rules. The modern state now has total control over law enforcement and punishment. The religious morals we should follow are voluntary and quite different from positive government laws which we must absolutely follow. Positive laws have legalized punishments based on the full force of the legal system.

Religious punishments evolved as consequences of breaking religious rules and the person experienced his punishment by not going to heaven and spending their days in hell or some other misery such as being reborn or reincarnated again as some kind of unwanted ugly pest. Today in almost all modern countries their legal punishments and religious punishments are very different. Religious punishments are mostly psychological and future driven such as going to hell, where legal punishments are more immediate and can be quite severe.

Culture Influence:

Having the Sabbath day off from work is one obvious cultural influence most of us experience and that had its start in religion. However, separating other cultural and religious traditions is at best complicated and difficult to decipher. Some would argue we know for sure religion influences our culture but at the same time our culture also influences our religions. A great example of how culture has influenced religion is how the recent cultural trend to accept gay marriage has changed the religious outlook on such things. Also, it was not long ago practicing Catholics were not supposed to eat meat on Friday, but the culture eventually changed the old religious principle so it is now acceptable to eat meat on Friday, although the reversal of meat of Friday has never been officially sanctioned by the Vatican.

Religions have impacted culture by way of many of our current rituals. We all know about prayer vigils, funerals, weddings, baptisms, and holidays such as Christmas and Day of ARAFAH. Even the word holidays came from the long version of "holy days" from our past religious traditions.

Religion also influences such cultural items as what we wear, what we eat, and of course how we behave in public. Wearing a turban or a hajib are some of the most obvious examples of this cultural influence initiated by religion. Not eating pork is a less obvious example. Sometimes it becomes difficult to differentiate between culture and religion in many areas of the world. Suffice it to say culture and religion have great influence and obviously the influence does go both ways.

Human rights Influence:

This is a complex topic to decipher as the relationship between religion and human rights is somewhat obscure and has been extremely changeable. Over the centuries our religions have both supported violence, prejudice, and repression and eventually played an important part in reversing the trend by encouraging the recent fight for universal human rights. Thankfully these days more and more societies and their religions are accepting the human rights idea and pushing them forward as the most desirable way for all societies to advance all of humanity.

There is much debate as to whether we would be as far along to standing up for human rights as we are today without the insistence of organized religions. Many times in the past our various religions were the worst transgressors of human rights. So the current two-sided argument is whether our human rights theory is based on religious faith or did it progress as an autonomous movement completely independent of religion.

If you are staunchly rooted in a progressive religion you would say religion had much to do with entrenching basic human rights but there is not much evidence to support the theory. Many think human rights slowly came about through education and mass communication which helped to drum up support for fighting for human rights. The killing of George Floyd in America is a prime recent example that spurred on more civil rights action, over and above any religious support. Some suggest human rights was actually more of a political drive combined with strong willed activists like Martin Luther King, Mahatma Gandhi, Nelson Mandela, and so many others.

When human rights eventually became a popular issue with the voters the astute politicians, as they are often prone to do, jumped onto the band wagon and pushed forward the human rights issue to help solidify their political base. These days we are seeing some reversal of human rights as more extreme religious sects such as Christian Nationalism gains a stronger foothold in places like America. So again we are confronted with which came first; did politicians see it as a winning agenda for their religious base of voters and they just followed along or were they for it as a basic civic right and not involved just for political expediency.

Morals Influence:

In at least three of the most publicised religions, all of their followers are supposed to follow the 10 commandments as their primary religious text sternly demands. Therefore, if the commandments are strictly followed, their religion can be held responsible for upholding the morals of the followers and the country where they reside. Many of these same religions also have other "laws" or morals which are mainstays of their religion and these also encourage proper civility of all those affiliated with the particular religion. For the most part we can see religions can be appreciated for their affect on the morals of the societies where the religions are practiced by the majority of the populace.

In the Buddhist faith, as far as morality is concerned, it means to have restraint and discipline over your body and speech. This means the faithful must follow accepted standards and the five precepts of Buddhism. The followers must not cause distress to themselves or to others by having respect for fife, property and relationships. Specific country laws and social standards do not form the basis of Buddhist ethics or morals but the unchanging laws of nature are a key component or rules and not any specific biblical type of commandments. Buddhists follow these precepts voluntarily because they are useful ethics for the body, speech, and mind and not because they fear some punishment at the end of life.

Most of religion's morals seem to be logical extensions of our current accepted behaviour and of course various legal institutions. However, there is nothing preventing a nonbeliever from being a moral person without having a belief rooted in any current religion. Whether these moral traditions would be the norm today without our past organized religions as a starting base is probably doubtful but they are here now and no doubt would continue on, even if there were no further organized faiths guiding the process.

There are occasions where a country's strict religious following goes against all modern day principles of freedom, equality, and morality. These people have returned to an overly strict adherence to an outdated and misinterpreted religious concept. By doing this they are reversing hundreds of years of humanitarian progress, reverting back to some previous unworkable tenet of an outdated religious sect.

In Afghanistan we have all witnessed the weird enforcement of an incorrectly interpreted, old religious scripture. These anti freedom, overly strict Islamic rules, currently existing in today's Taliban ruled Afghanistan have unfortunately adversely affected and doomed the women of the country. Afghanistan women are now forced into slavery and not allowed to hold a job or to get an education. This is one recent example of the consequences of a religious belief gone appallingly backward and being severely distorted by a few supposedly righteous leaders.

The emergence of ISIS a few years ago is another ridiculous form of over the top religious' expression having no place in a modern world. The Islamic State called ISIS started as an extreme militant offshoot of Al Qaeda and became so radical and brutal even Al Qaeda disowned it as part of their group. ISIS took over large parts of war ravaged Iraq and Syria and declared they were a new caliphate or new country following strict Islamic rule. Convert to their form of Islam or die was their harsh motto to all others. Many countries eventually joined together and militarily defeated this ugly extremist group but the remnants of ISIS still unleash horrendous terror attacks inside many unsuspecting countries. Their tactics were so brutal such as beheadings, slavery, and even banning things like music and smoking they have lost much of their former moral and religious appeal. They are still considered a dangerous force in the world and there are many worldwide resources focused on trying to eliminate the continuing threat from ISIS. We have to ask, is ISIS a religion unto itself or just politics; it is not wanted nor is it supported by the majority of Muslims no matter which topic it falls under!

The previous two examples were from the Islamic religion, but now we are seeing he same type of extreme religious back sliding happening in Christianity here in the USA. The current push by evangelical Christian nationalists is the extreme version emanating from the Christian religion. If we are not watchful we will face a similar peril that has befallen Afghanistan. Freedom of religion will be done away with here in America except for born again white Christians! So you can now see how easily such extremes as the feared Taliban could easily come into being and America may yet suffer a similar fate if evangelicals get their way.

Dress codes Influence:

In old Victorian days in England it was considered shameful to have a woman accidentally show a bit of her bare ankle. Makes you wonder how these old-timers would react to topless beaches and thong bikini bottoms like Brazilian and European beaches now allow. There is little evidence to suggest religion had much effect on either of these two dress code extremes. The dress codes more reflected the morals and culture of the times, not specifically the local religious teachings.

Some suggest restrictive American laws regarding topless bathing and other such displays of outright femininity are distinct religious restraints brought forward from their old colonial puritan religion days. The difference between how Europe and America view this topless bathing topic is striking for sure and is partly because of past religious teachings.

One of the codes of Islam is for both men and women to modestly dress. The Quran states "the Arab women used to uncover their faces as slave women do, which was an invitation to men to look at them. So Allah commanded them to cover themselves with the hijabs and cover their faces with them."

Modern day dress in most countries more often reflects the trend for the younger generation to differentiate themselves from the previous generation, in other words to be seen as distinctly different from their parents. Churches can and do preach their version of dress codes, but individualism, especially from the young these days, usually will override any religious doctrine unless brutally enforced by the government such as what we constantly see in Islamic Iran.

Art Influence:

Right from its outset every religion has used art to explain the many worldly mysteries, embellish their creation stories, and to show the wonder of the gods they worshiped. Even a caveman wall art from 40,000 years ago seems to show a god like creature. Every known civilization has had a religion of sorts and right along with it they had art to show their version of divine forms and to tell or explain the many religious rules and fables.

As each new religion evolved, its expressive art was considered a wonderful tool to be used to spread the word. The paintings, statues, and drawings were an integral way to physically display the message, so art was used as a method to help explain and spread the religion. Artists were often sponsored by wealthy followers to help the sponsors appear more religious and often there was great competition to be the most "righteous" sponsor of art amongst the wealthy benefactors of most religions.

So did art influence religion or did religion influence art? The history of art and the history of religion are actually inseparable. Most certainly religion helped provide a living for some "starving" artists and religion probably exercised creative domain and censored or banned all images not approved by the religious leaders of the day. Without doubt, religion has been the catalyst and benefactor for art since the first religion came along.

Music Influence:
We all know, and many of us appreciate, the music constantly played around our annual Christmas holiday

time. Much of the music is just winter or holiday related but some great songs are religious hymns sung during holiday church services. Obviously religion has had a substantial impact on at least some of our music. Many of our greatest and most popular musical entertainers have produced religion oriented hits and some of our fantastic vocalists have gotten their starts by singing in church choirs or performing in church organized shows.

There is no comparable Muslim music on the same scale as Christian music. Many Muslims believe the Quran prohibits musical instruments and of course singing. Many others do not agree with this strict interpretation and at various times Muslim music has flourished, but usually in the privacy of their own homes and palaces to avoid any criticism from religious purists.

There are many forms of song used in Jewish religious services and ceremonies. In our modern world, songs sung or composed by Jewish artists are well known and some of the best musicals and symphonies were created by Jewish talent.

To answer in a general form, has religion influenced music the answer would be most definitely a "yes", at least where there is religious tolerance for it.

Architecture Influence:

For those of us here in America our largest cathedrals come quickly to mind as a great example of the religious influence on architecture. But these religious design influences go far back into mankind's recorded history. We are still unearthing foundations of grand religious temples from old extinct civilizations. Some of the oldest manmade structures still standing are religious temples, cathedrals, and other special places of worship.

The fancy well adorned religious structures were both a place of worship but also a place to display the status and power of a particular religion. They reflected how the local populace revered their faith and wanted to show it off to all those who came to conquer them or to peacefully visit. Some more recent religions shed the ostentatious architecture display and demanded plain and simple structures to facilitate calm and piety for the worshipers. It goes to show sometimes the specific belief of the faithful can influence the structures design but also the majestic grandeur of the structure itself can reinforce or stimulate our actual religious beliefs.

Some buildings created for purely religious purposes were so spectacular that quite often the religions of conquering nations would modify them to be used to suit their own beliefs. The most perfect example of this is the majestic old domed building called the Hagia Sophia built in 527 in Istanbul Turkey. It was the largest Christian church at the time and was an Orthodox

Christian church until the Muslims of the Ottoman Empire conquered the area and turned it into an Islamic mosque. There are also examples of Islamic mosques in Spain being converted into Christian churches when the Muslims were eventually defeated and driven out.

The intricately adorned temple at Angkor Wat Cambodia covers over 400 square km. and is considered the largest religious structure in the world. It was built between 1113 and 1150 and is a magnificent structure by any measure. It started out being built as a Hindu temple but was converted to a Buddhist temple shortly after completion when the local religion changed.

The 500-year old St. Peter's Basilica in Vatican City "Rome" is the largest church in the world and is a treasure trove of both art and history. Its classic dome design has influenced countless other structures throughout the world used for religious and nonreligious purposes such as in government buildings.

Many religious structures demanded the adaptation of radical new design advances in how the actual buildings were constructed. In Europe the flying buttresses required to support tall stone cathedral walls is a prime example of adaptation of science to fit the religious architecture. The huge domed roof of the Hagia Sophia in Istanbul, and the seemingly earthquake proof old wooden Shinto temples of Japan, are examples of how religious structures advanced both architectural design and modern engineering.

Racism (Slavery) Influence:

Both the old and new testament of the Bible accepts the reality of slavery and even somewhat endorses it! Sometimes slavery was outright religiously motivated because the African people's blackness was often wrongly associated with evil and evil had to be conquered. Unfortunately, many conquered people in the supposed "good old days", black or not, were automatically taken as slaves by the conquering invader.

In the old testament Moses tells the Israelites they should acquire and keep slaves. In the new testament Paul tells slaves to "obey your earthy masters". These religious documents were often referred to when justifying the keeping of slaves, especially in the American south before the civil war. In the past, the current major religions of the world did not create slavery but apparently did absolutely nothing to discourage the unholy activity.

In summary, we can appreciate the fact Religion has ultimately influenced war, government structure, laws and legal punishments, culture, human rights, morals, dress codes, art, music, architecture, and racism. Would all of these influences from religion have eventually occurred without past religious doctrine being demanded from the faithful, probably not, but we will never know for certain.

Despite all the above mentioned influences religion has had on society, the current disturbing trend is toward simple apathy or indifference about religion in general and a slow movement away from most types of organized religion. Why is this happening and why now? Has the preponderance of new creation science finally had an effect on our religious beliefs? Does disinterest or religious apathy push us away or is there some other factor driving the shift away from organized religion.

Is this weakening of religion following the other trends such as drifting away from organizations in general? Is complete distrust of religion following along just like the growing distrust in government and is this trend becoming universal? Could the preponderance of online social contact, online gaming entertainment and other such online activities be a hidden cause because people are now just too disengaged with each other and have fallen away from customary normal human social activities? Have these universal, so called "social internet programs", actually done the opposite and made us less sociable and therefore less interested in believing in a God or fully believing in anything.

Is this current accelerating disinterest in religion one of the causes suddenly driving the evangelical right-wing towards pushing their unwanted Christian Nationalism? Are they trying to save their religion they see is obviously loosing ground in the entire country? Trying to force your religious beliefs onto someone else most likely will not work and could even drive more middle of the road believers further away from organized religion entirely.

Are todays evangelicals currently in such a panic because America and American politicians seem to be from more diverse cultures and represent many other religions than Christianity. Does the slight dilution of pure white run politics scare the hell out of them? Have these obvious racist evangelicals finally put their racism out in the open instead of keeping it well hidden as they have in the past. Are we finally seeing the racist divide coming right out into the open and possibly starting a race war in America? Preserving white racism seems to be the ultimate evangelical goal and their so called Christian Nationalism is just a false front for their racist attitude towards other races and indeed other religions.

Will Trump succeed with the help of all the white Christian Nationalists and will he install a similar Nazi nationalist dictatorship just like Hitler did in Germany. It sure looks like a dictatorship will be the sad future for America. Your God better help us all if Trump wins, although God didn't do much to stop Hitler and Hitler caused well over 20 million deaths of innocent people.

How many innocent lives will Trump's misfits and hooligans take; the 5 deaths caused by the January 6th insurrection was just a small taste? Watch out America and you evangelicals had better be careful what you wish for!

Most Americans have no idea of the disaster waiting on the horizon if a dictator like Trump comes into power. Both sides to the issue are well armed and just waiting to see what the outcome will be in November 2024. It's going to be troubling times no matter who wins the 2024 election.

<u>Chapter 17</u>

Why can't we just do away with religion?

Many of today's agnostics preview the world's ongoing struggles and wonder "why can't we do away with religion altogether". Such a simple statement invokes an immediate response from almost everyone. Many disgruntled citizens agree with the statement to eliminate religion but most don't. Now in the age of modern science has religion actually outlived its usefulness?

From chapter 24 of my e-book "Why can't we" written in 2022.

<u>Why can't we</u> do away with religion altogether. Now the harsh "do away with religion statement" should really stir the pot! We should realize religion is sometimes the root cause of our problems and not the solution to them. Should the modern day human race just do away with the unnecessary superstitious religious belief in God completely? Wow there he goes again!!

When it comes to problems we encounter everyday there are many of us who believe it is all "just God's plan". Using this theory, they just float along not trying to change or correct the many issues we humans constantly face. One has to wonder do they think its just God's plan for us to destroy our own planet by creating a massive

Global Warming problem, most of us doubt it is truly God's intended plan!

Many of us think when a TV crew interviews a survivor of a disaster like an F5 tornado and she says "God was looking out for her that's why she is still alive", to make such a statement is just nuts. Meanwhile her family were all killed and her home completely destroyed. What kind of God works this way and why would you even think such stupid thoughts; someone or something was actually helping or looking out for just you? Most think the destruction and her surviving was not much divine help at all! The storm destroyed her home and killed her family and she was just flat out lucky to escape and that's all there was to her surviving the disaster; no magical unforeseen hand had anything to do with it!

There are at least 16 religions in the world with at least one million followers and they all think their religion is the only correct one. Christians, Jews, and Muslims all believe in the old testament. Muslims even believe there was a Jesus but he was a prophet not the saviour of the world. Many of the largest religions refer to Jesus as a holy man as well, but not a saviour. So we see all the world's religions are a confusing jumble of varying beliefs and ancient superstitions.

Some believe religion is the cause of many of todays problems. The European white race thought their religion was so superior to others they spent centuries trying to convert other races and even populations of whole continents to Christianity. White men thought their religion was so superior they tried to eradicate the language, history, and culture of most North American indigenous peoples. Some religions such as Muslim, Christian, and many others, also spent centuries trying to convert the people they had conquered. Communist governments have now spent about a century trying to downplay or completely eradicate religion within their countries but with only limited success.

Many of the so called loving, peaceful, religions have spent centuries at war with each other and even at war within factions of the same religion. We have seen wars between the Shiite and Sunni who are both Muslims and between Protestants and Catholics who are both Christians and on it goes. This all begs an answer to the current question, is religion still relevant in the 21st century and if it is, which one?

We now know for certain how mankind evolved and developed. We now know how the earth was created and how it also evolved. We now know the actual chemical building blocks of life itself and what DNA represents. We no longer have to rely on some fictitious unseen deity to explain these formally mysterious events and creations. Science has proven most of these issues beyond any reasonable doubt. Mankind evolved over several million years through four distinct phases to the point where we are today. We were not magically manufactured in an instant as religion would have you believe. The planet itself evolved over 4.5 billion years and was not magically created in six days. These are the main divisions of human beliefs forming the two main creation theories of today and they are referred to as the Evolutionary Theory based on science and the religious version of Intelligent Design by some God.

The Big Bang some 13.819 billion years ago seems logical as a start for our current universe and our Milky Way galaxy, and eventually our Solar System. But some scientists speculate the current expansion and the eventual contracting of all the "stuff" in space have been happening over and over, big bang after big crunch, another big bang after big crunch, for longer than we humans could even measure, like eternity? In other words, our planet and we as a species are just an historic anomaly in the entire fabric of time, never having a start and never having an end. Nothing was created by a God, it has just always been here in one form or another. That's a hard concept for us to contemplate because we humans personally and naturally relate to starts and finishes of everything. Life and death, sun rise and sun set, the 4 seasons, etc., we are preconditioned to look for the beginning and the end of everything.

We now know when our planet and our sun will end (about 4 billion years from now), but what follows. Maybe our universe and possibly other universes have always existed and always will, even for trillions of our relatively short earth years. Could universes be created by big bangs and destroyed into black holes (big crunch) over and over again; there is no scientific reason why it is not possible. Matter, or its building blocks, contracts, or expands; it changes over and over, and never actually disappears. Not likely scientists will ever be able to definitively establish, let alone prove, this rebirth repetition cycle does occur, but it's fun to think about anyway. Agnostics don't believe a magical God created anything, the elements that make up matter have just always been here in one form or another and always will, and that's it!!!

Over the past 4.5 billion years, were we just the final outcome of hundreds of lucky timely breaks such as oxygen creation, water creation and stabilization, thin protective layers of atmosphere, carbon based life formation from single cells, Goldie Locks distance from our star and our planet's unique proximity to other larger protective planets? The early Earth survived and was aided by three nearby supernovas and also a collision with another planet which created our stabilizing moon. If any one of these and many other major occurrences did not manifest itself when it did, we humans and probably this planet could not exist as it does today. We ask, did some fictional God play a part in all these astrological episodes over the past 4.5 billion years or was it just the normal progression of chemistry and physics naturally proceeding throughout the development of our entire universe. Most of us will remain entrenched in either the evolutionary theory or the intelligent design theory and will never be convinced to change our beliefs.

We humans still use religious beliefs as an excuse to start wars and ferment hatred, especially when a charismatic leader ultimately gains influence and seizes power and can control the masses to do his evil will. One has to laugh at the ridiculous church services held at the frontlines of most wars where each combatant is actually praying to the same God to support their particular side in the conflict. Don't you think, if there was a human loving God, he would not allow war to start between his followers in the first place.

So when we ask **_why can't we_** realize religion is actually not needed any longer so why have it, you can not get a logical answer, because there is none. If there is no God and therefore no heaven and no eternal life, we must ask what's the point of us being here? That's probably the real question!

With all the scientific knowledge we now have about space and the creation of stars and our own planet and the previously stated negative opinion on religion, we can obviously morph into the big philosophical question "what's the point of it all". In other words, why are we here? We are just like other mammals, we're born, live for a while, procreate, and die. Without a hypothetical "prize" at the end, like heaven, there seems little point in us being here and while we are here we just use our intelligence to destroy our planet we rely on for life itself. However, unlike a pig, bird, spider, worm, or fish etc. we humans have the intelligence to ask such a question as "why are we here"?

Statistics shows us with the hundreds of billions or maybe even trillions of stars out there in our universe many billions of planets are also possible. With so many planets out there the odds are in favor of other possible life forms also existing somewhere else in the universe. What is the answer to all of our fortunate breaks which eventually created our planet and us humans and gives us the ability to ask the question, WHY are we each here? This simple question has tormented the great philosophers for centuries. If ET landed here today and saw us, what would they think is the reason for our existence? We suppose the answer would be the same as to why are they existing as well, no one knows why, probably just fate. Like being in the right place at the right time, at least for the time being.

That prompts one other comment about religion. If an Extraterrestrial ET did come visit us will our religions say "well God must have created them as well", how else could they explain a new being who was not created in "his image", or would it finally show what a big con religion has been all along? How would we earthlings handle such a new extraterrestrial revelation? Would religions fade away or be stronger than ever, now that's an interesting point to contemplate!

So when we asked "***Why can't we*** do away with religion altogether" it invoked an immediate response from almost everyone. Many agree with the statement to eliminate religion but most don't. Now in the age of modern science has religion outlived its usefulness? You can definitely have fun with the do away with religion question no matter who you ask!

The preceding was the chapter on religion from my book "Why Can't We".

Chapter 18

Do Dying People Just Hedge Their Bets:

If you believe simply asking for forgiveness will get you into heaven, do you just wait until you get older to return to your former religion and finally ask for forgiveness? Why are there mostly older people in your church these days? Was the delay in accepting religion initially their life plan or does the fear of death, that's just around the corner, suddenly reawaken their long dormant religious faith?

Some older people obviously think it makes sense to believe in religion so they try hard to believe in God, even if deep down they are convinced he does not exist. This now brings up a personal integrity issue because these people have corrupted their true beliefs just for an offhand chance they might fool God and go to heaven, if there is one.

Why are there so many nonbelievers? Many people believe God punishes all nonbelievers unjustly no matter what their circumstance. As shown elsewhere many nonbelievers have fallen victim to distasteful past interactions with the overly sanctimonious faithful who, by blatantly expressing their phoney righteousness, finally drive the nonbeliever away from any faith. Some nonbelievers are just not educated in the various forms of religion so they have not had a chance to properly choose. Others just don't have the intelligence to decide one way or the other. Therefore, it is seemingly impossible to force nonbelievers to accept something they may not even be aware of or if aware they are certain the basic premise of the religious belief is illogical.

The evangelicals now want their religion, and their GOP government, to force everyone to accept, on blind faith alone, in an entity the nonbeliever might not even be familiar. If the nonbeliever is familiar with the evangelical form of religion they may simply and completely disagree with their supreme God premise. Some righteous sanctimonious evangelicals believe they are actually exemplary Christians when they are far from achieving the desired lofty goal.

What about people trying to believe but just can't accept the premise of a supreme being? Is it possible for a person to force themselves to believe in God, such as when they are near the end of their life, not likely! What do they do now, just pretend to believe as sort of a personal insurance plan?

What would an agnostic person do, if when they die and they suddenly show up at the pearly gates to face a God they never believed existed? That's how religious people would probably frame your journey if you are a nonbeliever after you die. The religious person would say to you, once you're already at heaven's gates it is obviously too late to say "whoops I guess I was wrong", so is this the reason many older people try to redress their past nonreligious life style and rekindle religion again; is their return to religion simply a matter of stacking the future deck "just in case". Remember a true agnostic believes when you are dead, you are dead, there is no soul, and for sure no afterlife is possible so therefore no reason to "hedge your bet".

<u>Chapter 19</u>

The Final Decision for <u>No God</u>:

In the final determination it would seem religion basically breaks down into one simple decision, do you believe in God or do you firmly believe there is No God. If you chose the No God option, from the decision day onward, your life here on earth would seem to be pretty simple. You have made a choice and would seem to be done with it, however you are constantly confronted with subtle minor societal choices impacted by the various religions other people follow.

Many of our modern day ceremonies are based on ancient religious rituals. Should you, if you are an agnostic, attend these predominately religious ceremonies such as weddings, funerals, and baptisms? If you go to these ceremonies and stand or kneel for their prayer are you being two-faced or blasphemous, are you being sacrilegious? How do you handle religious family celebrations like Christmas, Easter, Ramadan, Chanukah or Passover? If you are testifying in a courtroom and have to swear an oath on the Bible ending with the words "So Help Me God", do you swear to an oath you don't believe in? If you are a sports fan at a NASCAR race and they give a prayer before dropping the green flag, do you stand and bow your head and remove your hat in respect and reverence; are you a fraud and imposter if you do? If you are leaving your Uber driver's car and he says "God be with you", how do you react, do you just say thank you and move on? It is difficult to escape these and many other religious interactions when you live in a predominately multi religious world and these religious exchanges can be extremely annoying if you are a devout agnostic.

What if you are religious but not of the Christian faith and someone is giving a prayer to God and Jesus but you are a Muslin, Hindu, Shinto, Jewish, First Nation, or one of the many other religions, what is your reaction? It is pretty selfish to think because you are a Christian, somehow it gives you the right to ignore all the other religions around you. How would you, if you were a Christian, react if you were visiting in a predominately Hindu neighborhood and had to listen to a Hindu prayer at your kid's ballgame? Not so simple when the shoe is on the other foot, is it?

A nonbeliever watching a professional baseball game sees the next batter come out to the on-deck circle and looking skyward says a quick prayer while making the sign of the cross before he steps up to bat and he quickly strikes out. We watch the relief pitcher look skyward, kiss the cross he has hung around his neck, and do the sign of the cross just before he delivers a disastrous basses loaded home run. To us agnostics it all just looks so useless and futile and sorry to say sometimes it is quite a comical ritual they go through just to express their religion while playing their sport. Usually the end result is not what they were obviously praying for in the first place.

The previously stated proposal suggesting we should do away with religion altogether brings up a similar thought about governments. Christian Nationalism or indeed any nationalism is also a very dividing force for us humans. Constant and never ending warfare has proven this fact! Albert Einstein is quoted as saying "Nationalism is an infantile disease. It is the measles of mankind". We now have to ask "what about giving up country designations as well". Think about it! We humans probably have less than a few hundred years remaining before the planet becomes uninhabitable for humanity because of our total disregard for the environment. Hundreds of years from now seems like a long time off in the future but it only took us about 150 years to already screw up the planet's temperature so it is not likely we will come remotely close to living here another few hundred years let alone another thousand years. We had best find a more competent method to work as a single unified group to save the planet we all live on, or we humans are probably doomed!

In the mean time we risk not even making it to 2027 because we are recklessly overheating the planet. That is the latest unnerving estimate from the head of the

United Nations climate agency. He says, regarding Global Warming, that "humanity has only two years left to save the world by making dramatic changes". We must eliminate the way we humans spew heat trapping emissions into our atmosphere or we will face irreversible changes on the entire planet.

We also face huge problems regarding over population, food insecurity, fresh water availability, and the obvious extreme climate disasters originating from Global Warming. Would not the world be much better off if we tackled all these issues as a unified group of humans and did away with our artificial divisions based on political party, religion, or nationality.

Being a white, born again, Christian American will not help one single bit if we as a group of humans can not solve all these important problems as a unified entity. The evangelical Christian Nationalists will never be able to accomplish anything on their own so they had better join with others to help solve our major world problems. Alienating all other races, religions, and nationalities will not help the situation we now face! All these worldly issues almost demand we tackle them as one unified body and not individual isolationist countries or specific independent religious entities. Face facts here people, God will not fix the Global Warming problem for us, it is now entirely up to us to correct the mess we ourselves created!

What if you are so uncertain about God's existence and you can not decide one way or the other? Maybe there is a God or maybe there is no God, you simply can't decide! Does your indecision or weak faith really mean you are in the No God side of the ledger or does your quiet questioning put you slightly over into the yes there is a God group? It is possible there are many people in this "undecided group" who seem to have no way out, but they keep their indecision about religion quietly to themselves?

As stated previously, religions are a terrible dividing force in our world and always have been. Would it not be simpler to have no God and enjoy the peace it brings for everyone?

Chapter 20

The Final Decision for <u>there is a God</u>:

Now on the other hand if you chose to believe there is a God, you have probably already decided which religion to believe in, or have you? Are you 100% certain you picked the right one? Does God even care which religion you follow or is He just satisfied you believe? Is making the correct choice about a religious denomination even an issue? If picking the exact spot-on religion is vitally important to you, does selecting and making the right choice overly complicate your eventual personal decision?

Then again, imagine you grew up in a society where no God or religion was even mentioned and on your 18th birthday you went out into the modern world. Suddenly you are confronted with a world full of religions you knew nothing about, what do you do? Some would suggest you would be greatly influenced by the society into which you were suddenly immersed. Let's say you found yourself in a small town in the American bible belt and only Baptist churches existed, it would be a logical assumption you would end up taking up their Baptist religion. Yet deep down in your psyche you might feel more like a Hindu or Buddhist in your overall outlook on life and not a true Baptist.

What if you knew nothing about religion and were suddenly deposited into the world's most cosmopolitan city such as Toronto Canada where every conceivable ethnic group and their churches were on full display. There are 120 Catholic churches, 133 United churches, almost 100 Jewish Synagogues, over 70 Mosques, and many hundreds more religious structures from every imaginable faith in the Greater Toronto area. Not knowing anything about religion how do you even begin to select one specific religion, the choice is so overwhelming? We can deduce from these two simple examples the religion you are now part of had to be compelled on you by your family, spouse, friends, or other peer influences. You don't just wake up one day and out of the clear blue say to yourself "I think will become a Baha' or a Tenrikyo or a Catholic" today.

So believing in a God is only the first problem you face. Whose God or which God is the next question? Which form of religion makes the most sense to you? Finally, which one of their denominations within the selected religion best fits your needs? What if you believe there is a God but make the wrong religion choice, where does it leave you on judgement day? A bit perplexing is it not?

Evangelical issues:
Be warned, going in whole hog into a radical religion like Christian evangelicalism can lead to other

problems. As we have seen it is not a big step from being a diehard evangelical to next joining a militant white Christian Nationalist cult.

When an evangelical is confronted with a doubter's difficult questions, that the evangelical obviously can not refute, they often respond with the stupid statement "it is just the devil talking thru you". They quickly shut you off because they have no logical rebuttal for your specific doubts or your superb questions. This can eventually lead to family breakups with other Christian or other nonbeliever relatives because the evangelical will ostracise all those they feel are now anti-Christ. Long standing, great family relationships can be destroyed because of the radical version of religion the new evangelical person chose to follow!

If they can drop or disavow previously close family members all in the name of their religion, we can see how easily they could attach their cause and themselves to an unchristian moron like Trump. They have made some personal mental excuse to simply disregard his many moral shortcomings because they think they need him in their struggle for religious dominance over all of America. Following a liar and mentally stunted man like Trump is a foolhardy decision by any sane person's estimation! Just ask all those who went to prison for their role in the January 6th insurrection whether believing his lies was worth the price they had to pay. Is it any surprise why those of us looking in from the outside wonder what the hell is wrong with these evangelical people?

God:

Something not discussed yet is what do you consider a God to be. We have not described what a God actually is or what form of relationship he has with humans. Again we can find volumes of supposed data describing Him but how factual is this divine reality evidence. During the course of our history many religious scholars proposed and are still proposing new theories trying to formulate this connection between God and to our world. So do we try to define what is a God or do we concentrate on what is his relationship with us humans? So does God look like what an artist portrays him to be or does it really matter? Is the connection to us the most important aspect of a God because we all see him in a different manner? It all comes down to what God means to you and how you portray that image in your own mind and nothing more!

Evil:

The one thing not mentioned in all of our previous discussions is what about the idea of a devil or Satan. Satan actually only comes into play if you are a religious person. Agnostics obviously do not have this mythical character as the opposing chess piece in the overall religious game. The religious premise of one supreme God must have this terrible unseen enemy called Satan to function as intended; God on one side and Satan on the other, in the never ending battle for your soul.

Most often someone who is described as evil or the devil incarnate is merely a person who is mentally deficient in some aspect of his personality. We all know in layman's terms Hitler was just plain crazy. Murders such as Ted Bundy, John Gacy, Charles Manson, and tyrants like Hitler, Pol Pot, Stalin, and Trump have no feeling of empathy towards other humans so inflicting incredible cruelty on others does not bother them at all. These murderers and dictators are morally and ethically corrupt from an early age. Trump has expressed similar inappropriate social behavior such as openly mocking a man with muscular dystrophy and worse than that he disrespected our fallen WW2 soldiers calling them all losers. Trump's consistent narcissistic and antisocial behavior have led many experts to suggest a diagnosis of malignant narcissism. He sees himself as the king of America or at a minimum he wants to be the dictator to rule until he dies. Watch out America, thanks to evangelicals the weird aspiration of Trump to have total domination of the USA is very close to becoming a reality.

So is there evil in the world or just very mentally sick humans. Agnostics don't need Satan to offset God's presence which gives a very different aspect to how they view bad people in the world. There is no battle for your soul because to them the soul doesn't exist.

Community of religion:

All the above is a fairly bland clinical approach to decipher religion and all its various nuances. Perhaps we have missed one of the most significant reasons for turning to religion in the first place and that would be the need for personal companionship or a sense of community. We have to ask, do humans actually have this need for "religious community" or "fellowship"? Many humans seem to have an inherent requirement to belong to something that provides them close association and for some reason belonging to an organized religion seems to fill the void. It could be a carry over from the old caveman days when there was safety in numbers and an obvious survival technique was to group together for support and needed protection. Something very special to them is required, it is some inherent need they have which obviously drives them to have faith in an unseen entity like a God!

Religion can fill this void for many people and can be a psychological life saviour for many. Many religious people find there is a need for religion to promote their newly found heathy behavior and they would not be able to function normally without their strong faith. It gives many people some social solidarity, mental peace, hope, friendships, and provides a real meaning in their life. That's all well and good, if people need this religious crutch to live a happy life so be it, just don't try to shove it down everyone else's throat like the evangelicals want to do! Obviously agnostics do not seem to have this same desire or they have found different methods to satisfy the need that religion seems to provide for so many.

Chapter 21

Some final Thoughts:

When this book was started there had not been any consideration into all the ramifications of delving fairly deep into most of the world's religions. It ended up being an overwhelming trip through history and it became a critical study of how religion has influenced and defined humanity for thousands of years. As was written above, religion has ultimately influenced war, government structure, laws, legal punishments, culture, human rights, morals, dress codes, art, music, architecture, and racism. Now many of us have to wonder "in a modern, well educated, and scientific oriented world is participating in an ancient superstition driven religion still relevant"? Do agnostics who firmly believe there is no God actually have it correct?

Think of humanities massive increase in knowledge and expertise in the current time frame and compare it to a few hundred years ago. As an example, humans have retrieved a sample of material from and asteroid that was two hundred million miles away from earth. As described previously, think about the complicated calculations involved to launch the Japanese rocket and hit such a small fast moving target so far away. It would be like shooting a pilot in the eye while he flew a jet fighter over Hawaii, while you were on the back of a flatbed truck traveling across the desert in Arizona, all while you were sitting on a moving merry-go-round.

Complicated just does not even begin to describe the difficulty involved in such an endeavor. It took our rocket about 3.5 years to travel the distance to the 1-kilometre wide spinning rock asteroid, land on it, collect a sample, and launch from it to return to earth. In total the unmanned space craft traveled 3.25 billion miles over 6 years. What us humans actually accomplished was a truly amazing technological feat to say the least. Did God help or did we do it all on our own without any divine help. If you believe there was a God helping in this enormous technical effort was it the Japanese Shinto God or yours?

We also ask "Can you believe in a God without joining a particular faith"? Do you consider yourself religious if you believe in a God but never pray or attend his place of worship as most religions demand? The liar Trump has said he believes in God but unless he figures a golf course is a church, we never actually see him attend a real church! So is he to be considered worthy of representing the Christian Nationalists or any Christians for that matter, definitely not by most people's judgement; Trump has just conned every evangelical as usual.

If you believe in a supreme God, which one of the 20 or so main religions do you think is best. Which one of the almost 4,000 minor variations of religion do you think is the right one for you? It would seem the easiest decision is to go with no God, keeping it simple.

Sitting here and reading what has been written and reflecting on what has been presented, it seems Buddhism seems to fit the author's current approach to religion more than anything else. Buddhism is more of a philosophy or a way of life and not a religion as we usually define them. It is a love of wisdom and you must lead a moral life, be mindful of your thoughts and actions, and continually develop wisdom and understanding. You can be an agnostic and a Buddhist at the same time because they have beliefs or a life philosophy which more closely match how the Buddhism religion represents life and Buddhists have no supreme all powerful God.

That was a fantastic personal revelation; actually adhering to some tenets of a religion without actually knowing it was being followed? Although corresponding to what was said above, Buddhism is more a life philosophy than a formal religion. Unknowingly taking Buddha's suggested path to end suffering and following the *"Noble Eightfold Path"* without even realizing it, was how many of us agnostics were already living life.

However, by not practicing Buddha's meditation principles you would not be considered a true Buddhist. Maybe a more thorough investigation into this philosophy is required. Doing all the right things expected of humans by our modern society and not believing in a supreme being pretty much makes you a Buddhist or at least you are closer to the Buddhist Religion or their philosophy of life than any of the others. If you want to review the Buddhist approach more fully you can return to chapter 10 above.

Chapter 22

? (the final big question)

If you are religious how would you answer the most perplexing **big question** "If God created everything, who created God"? I bet no one has ever asked you that!

If you are a religious person your answer is most likely "He has always been here"! Now where exactly "here" is remains another perplexing question. Is it only here on Earth, or just here in our Solar System, possibly just here in our Galaxy, or is here the entire Universe? The Bible states, He created everything so we have to assume creation must mean the entire universe including trillions of other stars and planets. Pretty impressive and formidable stuff, even for an all powerful God.

Anyway, the most likely agnostic rebuttal answer would be "If God must have always existed, why can't all the physical matter or all the other stuff in space have always existed as well"?

Why must we always revert to "how was it created"? Why couldn't all matter have just always existed. In other words, all the material that makes up matter in the entire universe apparently has always existed in one form or another. What makes physical creation such a universal law stating everything, every atom, had to be created by some magical being and not have simply always existed in one physical form or another. Humanities fascination with this creation theory is briefly explained above in chapter 17.

We know the earth came into existence by evolving from a mass of cosmic material which originally started out from the Big Bang. Is it not possible the last Big Bang was just the most recent in a never ending cycle of expansion and eventual contraction of all the matter in the universe occurring over and over again. Could all this matter from the last big bang eventually slow down and finally stop moving out into space and then the gravitational forces begin a reverse direction until it all combines again in one colossal black hole and the rebirth cycle of the universe starts all over again. This never ending cycle of space contraction and expansion takes possibly trillions of our extremely short earth years and has been going on in our universe forever. There was no actual creation for all of the stuff in space and it will never truly disappear, it just changes form and structure and reappears over and over in perpetuity. In other words, it is timeless.

So does this new explanation do away with the need for a creator God, many believe it does. In the overall trillions of years, the stars and planets in our universe have been coming into existence and eventually disappearing back into a black hole, we humans are a mere one second footnote in its overall time scale. The million or so years we have been around on earth is barely a blink of an eye in the overall history of our massive universe. Our small insignificant planet came into being about 4 billion years ago and will cease to exist in another 4 billion years from now. Right now other stars and planets are slowly being created from clouds of space dust and cosmic matter that are still combining together way out there in the not so empty reaches of space.

Think about it this way. Is *faithfully* believing in an unproven theory that all matter has always existed really any different than *faithfully* believing in an unproven creationist God. So far you can't definitively prove either assumption!

Are we special?

This brings up another interesting question. Why do we humans think we here on earth are so special? Most likely there are other life forms somewhere out in space existing right now and almost certainly there will be many more that will come into existence over the future of the vast universe. The latest best scientific estimate is there are 36 possible planets similar to Earth that could sustain a life form and that number is just in our one galaxy. So far we have not been able to accurately count how many galaxies there are out in the universe but the number is in the hundreds of billions.

Our small nondescript planet and of course we humans are probably just a minor biological exception with no particular relevance, nothing overly special, and our existence is possibly one of many throughout the expansive universe! Some extra-terrestrials may be more advanced than us, some will not be as highly developed. Thinking about the massive size of the universe makes you feel pretty insignificant doesn't it? Believing in God or no God we really are basically irrelevant in the whole scheme of the vast universe!

So agnostics have to state again, enjoy the life you now have because when it's over, it actually is over!

Chapter 23

Summary:

In the above pages the author has explained religion from primarily an agnostic's point of view. Including why we humans have held onto old superstitious religions and also where and why they originated in the first place. There is an explanation as to why many do not believe in a superior God and why so many others may have recently turned away from organized religion.

There was a definition of what separates nonbelievers from believers. The various differences that believers in God have and the overall approach to their own brand of religion was defined. The 5 largest religions are brought into sharp focus and their major divisions interpreted.

The two vary different creation theories are explored. Some of the other religious issues such a soul, spirits, angels, and afterlife were also defined. There is an attempt to explain why some seem to need a God to be personally fulfilled. Most of the consequential influences religions have had on mankind were stated and confirmed. The declaration that we really do not need organized religions any longer was proposed.

It was further shown how you can be a moral upright citizen without being religious. There was some effort to show how your life would be affected if you chose to believe there was no God and also how it would be affected if you decide there really is a God.

There was a special effort placed on trying to explain why America was established for many religions and not just one. Finally, a dire warning was issued to explain how, if Trump does get elected as America's first dictator, evangelical Christian nationalists will destroy America and with it America's promise of freedom of religion.

What if you decide incorrectly?
After all the long history of religion has been reviewed and the differences between being religious and nonreligious has been presented to you, it all comes back to the one all-important question, "do you have faith or not"? If you flat out state, you believe in a God you actually only have a 50% chance of being correct. Conversely, if you flat out state there is absolutely no God, you also only have a 50% chance of being correct. And remember, no one can prove you wrong no matter which way you chose!

The End

And peace be with you, no matter which way you lean!

This book was brought to you by the same author as the following books:

- **Are Americans Out of Touch with Reality**... how disinformation has destroyed the promise of America
- **Captain Jack, "Bush Pilot Mysteries"**.. a fun read about the adventures of a Canadian bush pilot
- **Canada Eh! Versus USA Y'all**.................. why Canada is the best place to live
- **Doomsdays and Global Warming**......... a must read for everyone!
- **Why Can't We?** .... a tongue in cheek look at fixing todays annoying problems, both large and small (e-book)
- **War Across the River**............................. the second American Civil War starting in 2025 (e-book)

Enjoy!